I THOUGHT IT
WAS GOD!

I THOUGHT IT WAS GOD!

DRU AXTEL

New Leaf Press
P.O. BOX 311, GREEN FOREST, AR 72638

FIRST EDITION
1988

Cover Photo: Mervin Reese Photographers
             Omaha, NB

Typesetting: A.G.A.P.E. Graphics & Printing
             Berryville, AR

Library of Congress Catalog Number: 88-62044
ISBN: 0-89221-160-1

CONTENTS

DEDICATION

To all the precious people who were involved with Born
Again Marriages and Marriage on the Rock. You are
my reason for this book.

To my kids, Kristin, Peter, and Mandy who love me 'no
matter what.' Without you being behind me all the way
I could not have written this book.

To Mom and Dad, to whom I gave many gray hairs. We
had some rough years but I thank them for giving me
all the love they had to give and my beloved childhood
on the farm.

To my 'burning bushes', Gavin and Patti MacLeod, Evelyn
Sherbondy, Robin and Cheryl Hancox who called me
throughout the darkest hours, refused to let me give up
or think of myself as a failure and kept insisting God
wanted me to write a book.

To Pastor Jim McGaffin, Pastor Tim Barnett, Pastor Ron
Blix, and Cliff Dudley who also encouraged me to write
and invested hours of their valuable time to counsel me.
In my search to correct any off doctrines I taught, their
understanding of the Scriptures always agreed although
these men do not know each other and did not realize I
always asked them all the same questions. The fact that
they would drop anything to let me cry, talk, or learn
from them truly kept me from going a little bit crazy.

To my best friend, Reta Hunt, who knows every detail of
my life forever and Mary Sumpter, who didn't know
me at all but both could hardly wait to read every
chapter as soon as I wrote it. Their enthusiasm and
support kept me writing.

May this book bring glory to You, God, and balance and
freedom in Jesus without compromise to those who read it.

PREFACE

I know many of you have wondered what has happened to me and the ministry. God has had me sort of hidden away in His 'intensive care' but I love you all and have longed to communicate with you.

I believe this is the Lord's desire also because He has provided me the opportunity to bare my soul to you along with the inspiration to do so when it would have been so much easier to just quietly fade away into oblivion and not risk controversy. I have tried to tell gut-wrenching things as frankly as I would if it were just you and me sitting in your living room. Some of it has been painful to reveal but I feel the very least I owe all of you who loved us is... the truth.

Dru Axtell

1
INNOCENCE

Weighing 105 pounds and 8 months pregnant, I glanced scornfully at myself in the mirror. "You look like an olive on a toothpick," I said to myself.

My ever-growing stomach mocked me day and night that I had turned out to be a bad girl just as my parents had constantly predicted from the time I was 14.

Still I felt it miserably unfair of God to make only the girl pay so dearly for a sin that two had committed.

Alone at night and fearful in a basement apartment in a strange city, I clutched my dog and tried to pretend the lump on my body was not a real baby that I had to give away but sort of a sickness that I would recover from in a few weeks.

Over and over, I contemplated my 21 years of life. I'd made a lot of mistakes before but never dreamed I would throw away everything I held dear to end up in such a bleak and hopeless condition.

Here I was...eating my heart out over my first husband who refused to reconcile with me, pregnant by a guy I didn't love, and married to a man I hardly knew!

"Dear God, help me! Forgive me. I'm so frightened!"

I had run away again just as I had dealt with other situations that I didn't know how to cope with, but this time, all my problems came with me. It was just as a friend of mine recently remarked to me, "Wherever I go, there I am!"

I thought back ruefully to that agonizing period of my life. I remember deciding back then I must not be nervous breakdown material or I'd surely have had one. An old cliche kept running through my mind . . . what was a nice girl like me doing in a place like this?

My life began on a small hundred-acre farm in Council Bluffs, Iowa. My dad raised corn, oats, soy beans, alfalfa, pigs, and cattle. I loved it and wanted to be a farmer but was determined to settle for being a farmer's wife since I had the misfortune of being born a girl. When I was four years old my folks decided to move to California because of Dad's sinus trouble. I can remember being horror stricken when they actually started putting sheets on the furniture, rolling up the rugs, and locking up our home. I hadn't seen much of city life, but I knew it meant I would have to play in a small yard or a playground covered with cement, and I wanted no part of it. Even at four, I remember loving our farm. I loved being able to run through the fields til I couldn't run any farther.

I hated California and was sick almost the entire time I was there. My mother somehow sensed that I wasn't physically sick but was homesick. The farm was bred into my dad, and soon, to my relief, we returned to Iowa and our farm, and I stopped throwing up. I never moved again until I got married.

My folks were married thirteen years and didn't think they could have children until I was born. Then twenty months later, my brother, Geoff, was born. He and I used to make houses under the branches in a grove of giant cedar trees. We had whatever cats were handy for kids. We'd pick vegetables out of the garden and make soup over a fire, but we always ended up fighting like cats and dogs. Mom would pick a switch off a tree and break it up. Geoff was very intellectual and never planned to be a farmer. He would stay inside and study, read, cook, and do scientific experiments.

Housework was boring to me; going outside to visit the newest batch of kittens, chicks or ducks was not. We even made pets out of pigs that the mother stepped on. Dad gave them to us to raise on a bottle, and they would get as tame as a puppy and come when we'd call them by name. It was agony to watch them go to the slaughter house.

I would do hard physical labor with my father and boy cousins. I learned to drive the tractor when I was six. As I grew older, I nearly killed myself loading bales of hay as big as the guys handled. We'd compare muscles. I enjoyed helping my dad from cleaning out pig pens to building fences. Nothing pleased me more than if Dad gave me a whole field to disk or harrow all by myself. It felt so good to be out in the fresh air knowing my dad counted me responsible enough to help with the spring planting.

I remember mornings before school my brother and I would get the milk bucket and run out to the pasture. Our cow was so tame, we'd sit the bucket under her while she grazed and each grab two "faucets". We got her milked in no time without having to put her in the barn.

My brother always had wires strung all over the house with his scientific experiments. Once he nearly electrocuted the preacher. He overheard my mother planning for Sunday company so he made a cushion for the iron lawn chair. He weaved it full of wires connected to an electric cord which ran into the house. My mother saw him heading to plug it in just as the preacher was going to sit in that chair and she stopped him just in time. My mother always thanked God that she caught him because that preacher died of a heart attack a few months later at forty-two. She thought he could have died in a lawn chair at our house.

We didn't have a television in those days and had to make our own entertainment. I never knew what to expect from my brother when he called, "Come out to the barn, Drusilla. I have something to show you."

I would either get shocked or a bucket of water would fall on my head. He was constantly thinking of some different trick to invent. I think I inherited it because my father was always inventing gadgets. He even patented one, and his father invented a hay fork that is in the Smithsonian Institute. I remember my mother's favorite nickname for my Dad was "Eli Whitney".

Our phone was on an eight-party line, and my brother rigged up speakers so you could hear the conversations out loud in the house. He also knew how to touch the wires together to make people get wrong numbers, and we would listen to their reactions. We would just crack up. Once he had one lady getting one wrong number after another. She began repeating each number out loud as she dialed it, trying to make certain she was dialing right. In hysterics, I finally begged my brother to let the lady get the right number so she wouldn't think she was going crazy.

My mother put up with my brother's wires and the scientific experiments and from me, she tolerated jars sitting all over the porch containing insects in various forms of development. I would find a big beautiful caterpillar, put it in a jar, and feed it until it made a chrysalis and hatched out into a moth or a butterfly. Usually they got loose and flew all over the house.

I also read voraciously. Dad drove us to town every Saturday, and I would come home with armloads of books from the public library. Books were a big part of my life because they would take me anywhere in the world. Dad didn't have money or time to take us on vacations but in books I could find out about other ways of life, people's hopes and dreams. My parents showered us with affection and praise. We didn't have much in material goods though, as Dad had a hard time making it. We were never poor, but we couldn't just go out and buy candy and pop. Those were special treats for birthdays and holidays. I would get a new dress for Christmas, Easter, and the opening day of school. The rest of the time my brother and I got the same jackets, jeans, flannel shirts, and boots. I would stuff my hair up in a baseball cap so we would look alike. Then people would say to my dad, when he took us to town, "What cute little twin boys you have!" I liked that because I thought I should have been a boy.

My dad played baseball with us each evening, and as a

result I was the only girl on our school team allowed to pitch. I really was a tom-boy.

We went to a one-room school house with eight grades and outdoor toilets. Being big for his age and very smart, my brother started first grade at four, so he was only a year behind me. My parents always praised us for our good grades but we knew they were expected of us. I don't remember ever getting anything but A's until I got to high school, and then I got a few B's. My brother and I were the only brother and sister honor roll team in high school the year I graduated.

I loved my family life as a child. My dad built my widowed grandma a small house on our farm. She was my only living grandparent and we all loved her very much. One of my earliest childhood memories is "Gram" playing *The Old Rugged Cross* and *In The Garden* on our piano while I sang at the top of my lungs. She taught me the words before I could read. My family never fought or quarreled. Relatives would come over, and my parents would have us line up and hug and kiss them hello and line up and hug and kiss them good-bye when they left. My mother's side of the family were English and French. Her grandfather fought in the civil war, escaped from Andersonville prison, rode in the pony express, owned a gold mine, and traveled in vaudeville. Hers was a colorful family leaning towards the arts.

Though my dad's side of the family were German and very stoic, my father was very affectionate. I think he decided to give us kids what he missed. I could climb up in his lap anytime, and he would tell me a story about himself as a little boy. Goodness, did he have stories. He grew up in the early 1900's. His dad had the first thrashing machine in the whole countryside. He and his brothers traveled around and hired out the machine. Once after eating lunch at a strange farm where they were thrashing, they found fresh cat skins nailed to a shed wall! Dad said they always carried candy bars after that. I was always wonderfully horrified by that story. My dad learned to drive one of the first cars invented. Driver's licenses were unheard of then. He used to laugh till the tears ran about nearly running over a traffic cop when he was fourteen. I was fascinated with my dad's childhood and worshipped the ground he walked on.

I'll never forget a lesson he taught me. We kids could use any of his tools as long as we cleaned them up and put them back in place. Once I accidentally broke a tool. I just knew I deserved a spanking. I sat and waited all day for Dad to come in out of the field, dreading that spanking. I knew he had no choice but to spank me. When he drove in on his tractor all dusty and tired, I ran and told him what I'd done. To my shock and amazement, he calmly went and mended the tool. I said, "Aren't you going to spank me?" He said, "No. If you always tell me the truth, I won't spank you. Besides, I know you didn't mean to." I really loved him for that.

We went to Sunday school and church every Sunday. I was in every Christmas play, lit candles for Sunday services, and was confirmed at thirteen. I talked to God as a child and would run through the fields just yelling up any little thought to Him. I read the Bible a lot and every time our little country church got a new preacher, I'd ask him about the Holy Spirit. At an early age, I sensed they had no more answers than I did. It was very discouraging. Even though Mom taught me to say my prayers every night in the name of Jesus, my family had never heard of being born-again. I talked to God every single day until I was about fifteen. Then I decided Jesus was a myth because I saw so much hypocrisy and refused to go to church with my parents anymore.

Mom was a kind and loving but very fearful person. She was also a martyr. She would do anything for her family. If she had corn for supper and I said I didn't like corn, she would get up and make me carrots. I would beg her not to bother, but she would anyway. That was the kind of woman she was: a wonderful cook and so concerned about feeding us kids well that she'd get up and make something else right in the middle of supper and let her own food get cold. She was totally devoted to my brother and me. Later in life her devotion began to be a pain. If I stayed out on a date too late, she would be waiting up in the window crying, "What did I ever do to deserve this?" and "What will the neighbors think about how late it was before you turned off the yard light?" That frustrated me because the nearest neighbors were half a mile away and I doubted that they sat up on Saturday nights to see how late our yard light was on. No parent should make their children their total source of happiness or reputation. It is too great a burden for any child to bear.

Almost every year it seemed like I had a new fear to contend with. One summer my dad was building a big metal machine shed. A severe windstorm took those pieces of corrugated tin and every stick of lumber and carried them all over the farm, totally destroying the building. We were huddled in the basement looking out the window. That day I became terrified of storms. If I would see black clouds building in the sky, I would worry that my dad wasn't going to get in out of the field in time. My mom would tease me, "Oh do you see a cloud in the sky? Are you afraid?" but she was the one who always dragged us to the cellar if it stormed.

To add to my fear, I constantly thought of one of the stories of my dad's childhood. His older brother was out plowing with a team of horses when a storm came, and he was hit by big pieces of hail and was struck by lightning which killed him. I feared that could happen to my father.

I was also afraid of a retarded cousin who lived a half a mile away. He was big and strong as an ox, and he would wander up and down the road grinding pebbles smooth between the palms of his hands. He had strokes of brilliance where he would remember the birthday and middle name of everybody he had ever met. Ten years later he could remember strangers' middle names. He liked little kids and he would set them on his lap and work their arms and legs like a doll. My mom told me that one time when dad was out in the field, my cousin picked her up and swung her in the air and carried her around, talking all the while about killing things. She knew that he could break her bones if he wanted to, and as a result she was scared to death of him. She pitied him but that didn't take away her fear when my father was working out in the field.

She taught my brother and me never to come into an empty house. One evening before we were born she had walked home from my aunt's house who was the mother of the retarded boy. She heard someone in our house and ran all the way back to my aunt's. In those days, tramps used to wander up from the railroad track. All summer long if I went in the house for a drink or back out in the yard to play, I had to lock the door behind me because my cousin could walk through the door at any time of the day. He could have yanked the door off the hinges but locking it would give us enough time to phone a neighbor man to come help. My aunt refused to put him in an institution. She told me Jesus appeared to her one day and gave her strength to keep him. No one knew his capabilities because he was so strong. He'd often wander in ranting and raving and cursing. When he was in a mood like that, we'd run for the house scared spitless. We'd refuse to unlock the door and my mother would yell at him to go home. After awhile he usually ambled off, and my heart finally slowed down. No one wanted to hurt my aunt's feelings and tell her to keep him home. My aunt would call my dad at times and say, "Help! He's chasing me. Please come quick!" So I grew up afraid of him, afraid of tramps coming if my dad was gone, and afraid ever to be alone.

During the polio epidemic, my brother contracted the disease on his tenth birthday. I remember seeing him rigid and hardly able to walk to the car to go to the hospital. I was terrified for him. The Salk vaccine had just come out, and the doctor asked if he could experiment on Geoff. My parents agreed. What did they have to lose? Every other little kid in the hospital was in an iron lung or in a wheelchair. My parents were worried sick. The vaccine worked, and within two weeks he was pushing the other kids in wheelchairs around the hospital corridors and turning pages of books for the kids in iron lungs. In three weeks he was playing baseball again! He has no side effects whatsoever. Our family regarded his recovery as an absolute miracle of God.

When I was about twelve years old, my parents had one big, super-colossal fight that threatened my security. My uncle, who was going through a divorce, began dating a lady and brought her out to meet my parents. My father hit the ceiling and said that was not moral. He wouldn't have such conduct on his property. My mother countered with, "Well, your sister did the same thing so how can you forbid my brother?"

They really went at it. I was more frightened than ever before in my life. My dad could get very verbal and extremely loud if he was mad about something. He could cut you to ribbons with words. Mom always gave in but that time she didn't and I actually feared that they were going to leave each other and get a divorce. Dad would sometimes talk about money being short and gripe that Mom spent too much or the cattle didn't bring what they should have, but I never thought of losing my home or not having enough to eat or not having both parents. All of a sudden all those things loomed up before me as real possibilities. I loved our farm and my family, and suddenly all that was threatened. Home and family were so valuable to me that at a very young age I perceived the horror of divorce and realized the harm it could do to kids and families. I ran from one to the other begging, "Daddy, please don't go. Mommy, please don't go. Promise me you won't go."

I loved them both and couldn't imagine my life without either one of them.

They would always say, "We won't go anywhere. We won't get a divorce. Don't worry."

I wasn't at all sure I could believe them, but part of me did because I knew how much they loved us kids. Sobbing frantically, I ran outside and hid until after dark. I hoped it was all over, but for about a six-month period, even though it seemed like six years when you are a kid, they didn't speak to one another and they didn't sleep in the same bed. My mother slept with me, and I resented it every night because it meant she wouldn't make up with my dad.

Friday evening at supper, the ritual went something like this: "Drusilla, please tell your mother that I'm going to town tomorrow morning at 10 o'clock if she wants to be ready." I wouldn't answer because I refused to be a part of their silly games. My mother would say, "Drusilla, tell your father I will be ready."

My mother didn't drive. She had had a terrible episode as a young woman. You didn't get a driver's license back in those days; you just learned to drive. She killed the motor on a railroad track and a train nearly hit her. From that day on,

---

17

Me in 5th grade with crooked, home-cut hair.

Geoff and me on one of our pet pigs.

Classmate Jeanne and me.

Me, 4 years.

My brother Geoff just home from Viet Nam
getting to know his first niece, Kristin.

Ethel Sherbondy and Harry Boehmn
on a date. This is my Mom and Dad.

Me, about 2½.

she never drove again. If we kids wanted to take dance lessons, piano lessons, or swimming lessons, we couldn't do it. Dad was too busy working to take us and Mom couldn't. Dad had wanted to be a doctor but his father wouldn't let him go past the 8th grade so I guess extra lessons seemed totally unnecessary to him. I think that is part of why I grew up feeling inferior. All my friends took lessons in this and that but I didn't get to. I never learned how to do anything except drive the tractor, do chores, cook, and sew.

One day my uncle who had been the object of the conflict came and played peacemaker. He told my folks he just couldn't stand to be at fault in their quarrel and begged them to make up. My dad was about to kick him off the place, but instead he let him in the door. I remember running outside and covering myself with a pile of fall leaves and huddling there like a scared rabbit until my uncle left. I just couldn't stand to hear fighting. No one said anything; it was like he hadn't even been there. The next day I overheard my mother explaining everything that had happened to my aunt on the phone. I heard her say, "Henry kissed me for the first time in six months this morning."

This was how I knew that they were all made up, but I never forgot the feeling of fear and insecurity. Years after that, if Dad ever raised his voice in anger over anything, those feelings loomed up as real as ever.

My mother valued art and was very creative. She won awards in high school for her drawings and water color paintings, and she even sold a few. I still admire her talent and have one of her paintings hanging in my home. She instilled a love of art in me and encouraged me to draw and paint.

My dad was the second youngest of ten kids. All of the others married nice farm girls and nice farm boys, but Dad married a city girl. She was the outcast of his family for years. Fifty years ago, she was looked upon as a foreigner because she decorated her home, talked, acted, thought, and even cooked differently. Thank God, by the time I was a teenager, they had all become more broad minded and were great friends.

We were taught that when company came, children were

to be seen and not heard. My folks made us get up and sing for people, though. If we could get away with it, my brother and I would run and hide because we knew we would have to perform, but we were not to participate in the conversation unless first addressed by an adult.

Once for a rare treat, my parents took us to a fair where a man named Johnny Maddox, known as "Crazy Otto," was playing ragtime. He became my brother's idol, and he begged to learn to play the piano. Finally my mother engaged a neighbor girl who drove past our house to high school to come once a week and give us piano lessons. My hands were too short to even reach an octave. I struggled and hated it. My brother has long fingers and took to it like a duck to water. Now when company came, I would sing and he would play. But after our little act was done, we were expected to sit down and be quiet. An interesting side light is that my brother now lives near Georgetown, VA. He discovered Johnny Maddox playing in a small restaurant there. He has become good friends with his childhood idol, and I think he plays ragtime piano just as well as Johnny Maddox.

Because my dad didn't want to spend money on frivolous things and my mother didn't want me to look too grown up, even though I was nearly a teenager, I never went to a beautician, never got a perm, and had homemade hair cuts that were crooked. In 6th grade, I started walking stoop-shouldered. Mom would tell me to stand up straight but I was self-conscious because she wouldn't buy me a bra. Finally, I saved up my allowance and bought one at the dime store. I had no idea about how to buy the right size so I had to go down to my grandmother's and use her sewing machine until I got it to fit me. She understood those things. I didn't have fancy clothes so I always felt inferior. To this day I hate my eighth-grade graduation picture of my classmate and I holding our diplomas. Her hair had been fixed at the beauty shop. Her dress was the perfect length. She wore nylons and her first pair of high-heels. I stood there with a homemade hair-do, hairy legs, anklets, and flats feeling painfully aware that I didn't look like the other girls although my mother said I looked adorable.

We kids were very sheltered all through childhood. On rare occasions, we went to a movie and if there was any violence or horror stuff, my mother covered my eyes. I remember specifically going to the mailbox one day and finding a *Ladies' Home Journal*. Glancing through it, I saw an article about VD listed on the front page. I thought, "I've got to read that. I wonder what VD is?"

I brought the mail in the house and forgot about the article until several days later. I picked up the magazine to see what on earth VD was and noticed that the article had been neatly clipped out. I knew from that, that I shouldn't ask my mother what VD was. It certainly must be something very bad, and my curiosity ran wild.

One day I was rummaging around in my mother's drawer looking for something and found a book underneath her clothes about how mothers were to tell daughters about having periods. When I was about eleven, Mom had tried to tell me what happened to girls when they grew up. She was so embarrassed that I got embarrassed and ran out of the room before she had finished! I went around thinking when I hit thirteen, I was going to have the "affliction" nonstop for the rest of my life! Until I found that book and read the end of the story, I thought for certain it was a curse to be a girl. What a relief!

Me about ten with latest batch of kittens.
(I'm wearing boy's jacket, jeans and boots!)

2
THE DIARY

In ninth grade I was faced with transferring from eight years in a one-room country schoolhouse with thirteen kids to city high with over a thousand kids. I was excited and scared spitless. I felt so self-conscious about not having a professional hairdo or nice clothes. My mother taught me how to sew when I was little and thank God, full skirts with as many starched petticoats as you could stuff under them were "in". I'd save up my allowance and buy four yards of material for a quarter a yard and make a new skirt and hope I didn't look too much different from the girls who bought theirs.

The summer before I entered high school, my aunt gave me a diary for my fourteenth birthday and said, "I would sure like to read this diary after you start dating."

I thought, "There probably won't be anything in it. Who is going to want to date me?"

In high school, I found a best friend. Her name was Kathy Jensen, and she was very sweet and pretty. I envied her because boys just flocked around her. I wondered why she would want me for a best friend. She lived down the road from me a few miles, and we did everything together. She helped me with my hair and makeup, I taught her how to drive the tractor, and we talked about boys. To this day, we are the best of friends.

In the second semester of my freshman year, the boy of my dreams came walking into my math class and sat down behind me. I took one look at him and knew he was "the one" ...just like *"Some Enchanted Evening."* His name was Jack. He was tall and good looking, and he would tease me all through math class. Math was easy for him, and he would help me with my problems. Once he had to do an essay but because of a job after school, he was afraid of not getting it done. I volunteered to write it for him and when I handed it to him, wonder upon wonders, he said, "Well, how about me taking you to a movie for this?" I went home with a lump in my throat for fear my folks wouldn't let me go, but since we were to double with his friend, Dan, and his date, they decided I could accept. I was in heaven. Kathy helped me plan what to wear. We went to a drive-in movie and ate pizza with cheese that strung all over as we shared it. The boys were funny all evening, and he held my hand.

This was the beginning of a summer like I had read about in all the teenage romance books I got at the library. He kissed me good-night on our third date while soft rain fell, and I thought my dreams had come true. Now when all the girls talked about kissing, I knew what it felt like too! I never thought any guy in the whole world would kiss me - let alone a dreamy one like this. At last . . . something too-good-to-be-true to write in my diary.

Jack introduced my best friend, Kathy, to his buddy, Dave. The four of us did everything together - including falling in love. I wrote it all in my diary because I had decided to be an author, and I felt that when I grew out of that once-in-a-lifetime experience, I might forget those "first love" feelings. Someday I was going to write a teenage romance novel like the ones I devoured from the public library, but this one would be true.

For the first time in my life, I began to feel popular. Jack was so handsome that I would notice girls turning around to stare at him. Some of the city girls I envied because of their clothes now envied me. He was two years older than me and not at all like most of the cute boys in school who were conceited - in fact, he had no idea he was that good looking so I liked him all the more. I was in love hook, line, and sinker.

I was allowed one date a week so in between Saturday nights, I would daydream. As summer went by, my mother began noticing and got really scared. She never talked to me about the facts of life so I was totally unprepared when, one day out of the blue, she asked me, "Do you ever take your clothes off around Jack?" I remember getting sick at my stomach because I was very modest and totally ignorant about sex. I couldn't figure out why she would ask such a dirty- minded question. I stammered out, "What would I do a thing like that for?" I meant every word of it. Remember, when I was growing up, we did not have blatant sex in movies and on T.V. "I Love Lucy" was about as sexy as you got in those days.

I really didn't know what she was getting at and couldn't see why she would want to make something dirty out of something so innocent and the most beautiful thing that had ever happened to me in my life. Jack was my prince and a perfect gentleman. At that time in my life, I didn't know about boys who tried to pressure girls into sex. We were just kids, and I think sex would've frightened us both. Everything was carefree and sweet - what had come over my mother?

She then asked me if I knew how girls got pregnant. I thought she had completely lost her mind because what did that have to do with anything? I mean, didn't God just make that happen when you got married? She then told me how, graphically and clinically, and I interrupted her and said, "I know all that!" and ran out of the house. Really I didn't, but out of sheer embarrassment I had lied to escape further discussion.

I decided to find out if my mother knew what she was talking about on my next visit to the public library. I heard kids talking about the famous Kinsey report which had just come out. You had to be an adult in order to check it out. I found it, crawled on my hands and knees to a hidden spot and read it. I was amazed! My mother was right!

My mother continued to be frightened, and one day she found my diary. In it she read about our going to the top of a bluff where all the kids used to go and park. There was a monument to Lewis and Clark's expedition there overlooking the Missouri River valley into Omaha, Nebraska. Towards the end of a Saturday night date, Jack and Dave would suggest going to "look at the 'purty' lights," and we would stand up there on the edge of the bluff and kiss in the moonlight. I wrote a detailed description of how beautiful it was and all the feelings in my heart. (Only my diary and Kathy knew of these feelings - I was far too bashful to tell them to Jack.) At any rate, I wanted to remember every detail for my book.

My mother brought my diary to me and said, "Dru, I just read this. You are far too young to be kissing. I never kissed a boy until I was engaged. This is pure trash, and I want you to burn it now. If you refuse, you can never see Jack again, and what's more, if you ever kiss him again, you can never see him either!"

I burned it. I remember hot, bitter tears as I watched each page go up in flames. How could my mother not understand? From then on, we weren't trusted to go off the farm. The boys would come out on Saturday night and eat pizza and drink Pepsi. I don't know how they ever stood it. One evening, the four of us were out in the lawn chairs, and I leaned over and kissed Jack on the cheek. All hell broke loose! My folks had been spying out the upstairs window. My father came storming out and yelled at my friends to get off the property. I would've gone with them, but he held me by my arms. In anguish, I watched through my tears as the dearest friends I ever had hurried to the car. Tires spun a shower of gravel against the garage door as they sped away. My father whom I had worshipped all my life suddenly became an ogre and my enemy. My folks then turned me into a literal prisoner. I could not receive any phone calls, and one of them held me by the arm when we went to town on Saturday. I spent the rest of the summer days walking in the fields through a blur of tears, crying out loud, "Daddy, what happened? Why don't you believe me? God, why is this happening to me?'' Once I walked through barbed wire and didn't even notice I'd cut my foot real bad until my mother screamed when I went in the house because she saw blood sloshing out of the top of my loafer. She wanted to take me to have stitches, but I glared at her with such cold contempt, she actually backed off. I have a bad scar on that foot to this day.

School would begin in a few weeks and my parents made me promise I wouldn't speak to any of my friends, or I couldn't go back to that school. My younger brother would be a freshman that year, and he was commissioned to report to my parents if I dared go near any of them. I turned into a liar then. I promised anything they wanted just to get to go back to school. In school, I'd write notes and get friends to smuggle them to Kathy, and that's how I kept in touch. Jack was afraid to speak to me for fear of getting me taken out of school by my parents. After a couple of months, he joined the Navy, at seventeen. I thought he must not love me anymore because of what my parents had done to him.

The day he was to leave I couldn't stand not to say goodbye. I lied to my father and said I needed some notebook paper. He dropped me off and waited for me at the back of Kressy's five and dime store. Knowing that I didn't have much time, I bolted through the store, ran as hard as I could up to the cafe a few blocks away where all the kids hung out after school. I ran up to Jack and blurted, ''Good luck, Jack,'' and ran back out sobbing hysterically. I didn't give him a chance to say a word. I was afraid he didn't care anymore but I didn't want to know for sure. Worn out and sobbing, I stopped to catch my breath in the doorway of a store. The owner came out and grabbed me asking, ''Young lady, is something wrong?'' I choked, ''Oh, nothing except a friend of mine is leaving for the Navy.'' I then continued my desperate run to the store where my father was waiting, grabbed some paper, paid for it in record time, wiped my eyes, and walked sedately out of the store to my father's car. I thought my insides would burst from the pain, but my father never knew.

Soon after he left, a girlfriend of one of Jack's buddies told me he wanted to break up with me. She said if I would date, it would set him free and she knew that was what he wanted. It never occurred to me to write him and ask him if that was true. I was so beaten down and humiliated by the conditions my parents had placed on me, I didn't blame him if he was tired of the entire situation. When another boy asked me out, I accepted, thinking if Jack doesn't want me anymore, it didn't matter who I went with. At least it got me out of the house.

My parents were thrilled thinking I had finally come to my senses and was over Jack. They were very nice to my new boyfriend and allowed me more freedom. The irony of it was that the thing they feared happening with Jack would've happened with this boy had I not fought him off constantly. I suddenly knew what my folks had been worried about, and I laughed bitterly to myself. I would have stopped going out with him because of his advances, but I thought it served my parents right. They drove the one I loved out of my life who was a gentlemen and let me date a guy who wouldn't keep his hands off me. I smiled at the irony of it all.

Suddenly without warning they changed. The night before the prom my date rode his bicycle out to visit me. My corsage was in the refrigerator, and my new formal was in the closet. That was one visit too many. My folks thought he was getting too serious and kicked him off the place and forbid me to go to the prom or to see him again. I was angry and frustrated. I could hardly believe it . . . not this again? I started thinking about leaving home as soon as I graduated.

One of my prayers was answered. Mom allowed me to be friends with Kathy again. One hot day the next summer I was helping my mother and grandmother can tomatoes, when Kathy called. She told me excitedly that Jack was home on leave and wanted to see me. My heart pounded wildly. I responded with a code word that meant my mother was right there so I couldn't talk openly. Then I said, "Oh, you want me to spend the night? I'd love to." I hated being deceitful, but I felt my parents were unreasonable and I had no other option.

Kathy's parents had never allowed her to date. She had only been able to see Dave at my house so they had not seen each other in a long time either. We said we were going to babysit and went to meet Jack and Dave. My heart sang just like old times. Jack told me the girl had lied to me about my dating other guys. She wanted Jack for herself. Before the night was over and we said our good-byes, Jack gave me his Navy ring. I was in heaven going steady with Jack again. I didn't dare let my folks know so Kathy kept his ring for me. When school started, I wore it and then left it in my locker. I wrote Jack during study hall, and he sent his letters to my girlfriend, Joann's house whose parents also thought mine were unreasonable.

My diary was a five-year one, and since I had burned only one year of it, I began writing in it again--only this time in code. One day when I came home from school, my mother was staring out the window with her back to me, and the atmosphere was like a deep freeze. "Dru, I have decoded your diary. I know that you and Jack are going steady, and if you are going to be that much of a rebel, I give up. You might as well date him openly and tell him to write you here at home." She spoke in a martyr tone of voice.

I was elated. I let my parents read all his letters, hoping if they got to know him, they would not be sorry that they had relented. Jack had taken his GED in the navy and passed with flying colors. He was learning to be a jet mechanic on an aircraft carrier. We went steady for the next two years, and I lived for the times he came home on leave. He was so handsome in his Navy uniform, and he treated me like a princess. My parents respected his achievements and soon genuinely liked him. I thought, "Miracles do happen!"

During my senior year, some of my friends began to convince me I shouldn't go steady with a guy stuck out in the middle of the ocean and miss out on all the fun of my last year in school. I didn't want to do anything to risk losing him, but to please my friends, I wrote Jack an experimental letter asking him how he felt about it. When I told my girlfriend I couldn't mail it, she said, "But I can," grabbed the letter out of my hand, ran, and put it into the nearby mailbox before I could catch her. I felt helpless. My fate had been taken out of my hands...literally.

29

A couple of weeks later a tall, skinny boy asked me out. I told him I was waiting for a guy in the Navy who I was going to marry but I would go to the game with him, just for fun. He said that was fine, and we began going to all the senior functions together.

This worked real well until the last half of the term. He and I had one class together. The teacher would hurry through the main subject and then teach us about sex. When he discovered that this boy and I were dating, he would use us as examples. He would say if we ever got married and wanted to have a baby, this is what we would do. Then in detail and very vividly he explained it step by step.

I would sit there with a flaming face, perspiration drenching my body. It was too humiliating for words to have the whole class thinking about this boy and I having, I couldn't say it, S-E-X! I didn't complain to my parents or anyone else because it was too embarrassing and a sore subject besides. Students didn't complain against teachers in those days, and I was too bashful to incur his wrath by walking out of class. This went on day after day, week after week. The boy I was dating had a job after school with older married men, and he would go to work and tell them what the teacher had said. They would get out their sex books and out do the teacher! Then we would go out on Saturday night, and he would tell me what they had said.

Jeanne and I holding
8th grade diplomas,
(hairy legs and flats for me

3
BURDEN OF GUILT

As the months went by, the class began to be very curious and lust was rampant. One night after looking through a book about sex that one of the guys had given my date, we began to experiment out of sheer curiosity. It certainly had nothing to do with love.

To experience the feeling the teacher couldn't quit talking about, I mean, you just had not lived until you knew what it was like according to him. It became an obsession to the class and I doubt that some of them fought it as long as I did.

When the fumbling became ridiculous, I woke up to what I was doing and realized I didn't want to be doing it. I yelled, "Stop, stop!" and he did. I thought the entire thing was a fiasco and thanked God I was still a virgin. But when I got home, I knew I wasn't!

I was frantic. Because of those few minutes of experimenting, I was ruined. I looked in the mirror to see if I looked any different. I felt that everyone I saw the next morning was going to take one look at me and say, "I know what you did last night." I felt so ashamed but all my regret couldn't undo it.

I didn't know God well enough to realize I had sinned against Him, but I knew for certain that I had sinned against Jack. I loved him and should have saved myself for him alone. To make matters worse, I was sure even if I never told him, he would find out some day and hate me. The teacher was emphatic that any guy could always tell if his girl was a virgin. This haunted me and I hated myself.

Guilt controlled much of my life from then on, and I began to dread the marriage day for which I had been living.

God seems to forgive us easier than we do ourselves.

After I graduated, I got a job as a stenographer at Northwestern Bell Telephone Company in Omaha, NB. I was thrilled that I was actually handling the responsibility of driving all the way to the big city of Omaha and earning my own money. I saved up enough to buy my first car and it was a humdinger, a customized 1949 Chevy, painted powder blue. I changed the name on its rear fenders from Road Hog to Blue Angel and felt like an uptown girl.

I dated a few guys very casually during that year. What else could it be when I spent most of the evening telling them about the sailor I was soon going to marry? I never could figure out why any of them ever called for the second date.

At last the long-awaited day approached for Jack to be discharged from the Navy. His parents, whom I loved very much, took me with them to Virginia Beach to pick him up. When we hit the Virginia border, I came to the edge of the seat and rode that way until we arrived. At the naval base there was such a sea of sailors getting off the ship that his mom said, "How are we ever going to find Jack? They all look alike." I scanned the faces and in moments spied him. His tanned face was so handsome, he stood out from all the rest. I watched him fight his way through the crowd to get to us, choking back happy tears. At last, his strong arms were around me. He swung me off my feet and hugged the breath out of me. Four years of waiting were over. Jack was free and we would live happily ever after. Nothing could ever mar this "Cinderella and Prince Charming" story. Surely all of the heartbreak stuff was behind us forever.

All the way home to Iowa, Jack never took his arm from

around me, whether he was riding or driving. I was inexpressibly happy. Away from home, all the old fears seemed to disappear. But when we reached Council Bluffs, and he put a diamond on my finger, everything suddenly seemed to change.

On one of our dates we ran into a fellow I had dated and he spoke to me. Jack became very jealous and seemed now to be angry all of the time. I had never seen him like this and concluded he was mad at me for dating and he "knew." Fear and guilt possessed me. Consequently, I could not be open or honest with him or be my real self. My dad gave us a down payment on a darling little house but the enchantment of furnishing it was dimmed by a cloud of fear that told me Jack really didn't love me and was marrying me to prove to everyone at home that he could have me.

Our wedding was beautiful but as we stood at the altar, a bizarre thing happened. A voice that no one else seemed to hear suddenly spoke in my ear, "If it doesn't work, you can always get a divorce!" the voice spoke this same thing over and over. I could hardly hear the preacher or thrill at the handsome groom by my side. All I could think about was this voice. I didn't know who or what it was, but I was scared all the way through my wedding which is supposed to be the most beautiful day in a girl's life.

We went to the Black Hills on our honeymoon. Once again, leaving our home town seemed to leave old fears and jealousies behind. I only knew I had no choice but to marry him because I loved him.

We got a little log cabin, built a cozy fire and toasted each other with champagne. But alas, there was trouble in paradise. In the middle of our wedding night, the room filled with smoke. Jack had forgotten to open the flue. Coughing and gasping for air, we threw open the windows and laughed and laughed while we almost choked. However, our laughter was soon to end.

I was greatly relieved that he hadn't said anything about my not being a virgin. I concluded he probably knew but either chose not to say anything or it didn't bother him. I desperately hoped that was the case and looked forward to setting up housekeeping in our dream house. But when we got home, it was as though a black cloud settled over us.

Jack liked to help people, and all his friends knew it. It seemed from the time we arrived home, someone called every evening for a favor. If it wasn't that, his buddies wanted to go out for a beer, and I found myself alone almost every night knowing for sure our honeymoon was over. I was scared to be alone in a strange house in the city for the first time in my life.

As soon as it would get dark, if Jack wasn't home, my heart would pound in fright. I would sit with the lights off watching out the front room window for him to come home. If I saw a shadowy figure cut through our yard, I would think it was a prowler. Night after night, I felt more rejected and unwanted. I became more and more angry at him for leaving me alone to face this fear. I never told him about my fear of being alone. I was to embarrassed and afraid he would just make fun of me.

Sometimes I would call a friend of his to see if they knew where he was, and they even began to say, "He is probably stepping out on you. I wouldn't take that if I were you, Dru."

As time went on, I decided they were right. Even though I felt I deserved this kind of treatment for what I had done, still I didn't think I could take much more. I wondered why in the world he had married me if he didn't want to be with me. Perhaps he was punishing me.

We began to quarrel, and I would cry myself to sleep at night. He threatened he was going to leave me and it would be easier for me if I left first. I would stare at him sleeping beside me, oblivious to all my tears, and think how handsome he was even in his sleep. I wondered how I could ever live without him. He had been a part of me for a third of my young life.

Now the voice reasoned with me, "I know you love him, but he doesn't love you, and you can't do without love all your life. It would be better to find someone you don't love as much but who loves you. Divorce him before he divorces you."

I finally went home to live with my parents. He would come and see me and ask me to tell him how to love me. I couldn't understand why, if he loved me, he didn't just treat me like he had all the years before we were married so I said, "If you have to ask me how, then you must not love me," which was no help at all. Looking back, I was very young, very guilty and very ignorant. I think I expected marriage to be one long romantic date. I actually thought he knew how he was hurting me but being so full of guilt, I didn't know how to communicate openly with him. Dear reader, NEVER expect your marriage partner to be a mind reader! I'm sure now this young husband of mine hadn't a clue as to what was the matter with me.

And never ASSUME you know what's going on in your partner's mind unless he tells you. Assumption is a low form of intelligence. Assumption, for the most part, cost me my marriage. I found out after it was too late that he was not angry with me all the time but overwhelmed with financial pressure. I had no idea the older married guys at work constantly jeered him, saying that if he was the boss of his own house, he had to prove it by staying out drinking with them. Neither did I find out that the friends who called me saying they "knew for certain" Jack was calling other girls had no real proof at all.

I did not get any of the true facts. What I DID get was an old boyfriend who heard I was miserable coming around for me to cry on his shoulder. He told me he had always loved me and was waiting for me. He knew it was a mistake for me to marry Jack because I didn't deserve to be treated this way.

Normally, I wouldn't have given this guy the time of day if Jack was anywhere in the vicinity, but, feeling sorry for myself, I thought he was terribly understanding and sympathetic. Now I had a lot of voices all urging me to get a divorce.

I left and went back to Jack three times. He seemed to grow angrier all the time. Finally, I couldn't take seeing my handsome prince frowning at me any longer, and I really couldn't take the yelling. I got as fearful as I did as a child when my Dad yelled. My guilt over cheating on him never left me. I was sure he knew and couldn't forgive me. I thought his anger was my sin mirrored on his face and, thinking it was impossible to ever undo what I had done, I let the divorce go through.

After the divorce, a girlfriend at work asked me to a YMCA dance. I began dating several nice-looking guys frantically trying to forget Jack. I couldn't do it. A few months later, he called me and we started dating again. It seems hindsight is always 20/20. No matter how bad our marriage had been, I had had a taste of life without the man I loved, and I didn't want any more of it. I desperately wanted another chance and hoped he did too. This time, I would not expect to be treated with kid gloves. Knowing he would come home to me sometime sure beat him not coming home to me at all.

At the same time, Kathy asked me to do her fiance a favor and go out with a friend of his who had just gotten in town. That was how I met Kent. The first thing he talked about was how much money he made. He bragged about all the guys he had working for him and what a good salesman he was. I thought he was conceited and didn't like him very well but went on a double-date waterskiing just to please Kathy.

Every other guy was just someone to kill time with in case Jack didn't call. I began begging him to come back to me. When I would do that, he wouldn't say anything; he'd just pound the steering wheel. Time after time, I'd beg and he'd just pound the steering wheel. I kept thinking, "Well, he looks at me like he cares for me and kisses don't lie. I know I've hurt him and his pride, but I'll hang in there. Surely we will get back together."

I used to sit staring at the phone willing it to ring. If Jack hadn't called by 10:00 p.m., I would sometimes go out with whoever had called earlier because I was so bored and lonely at home. One Sunday, Jack and I were supposed to go waterskiing with Kathy and her fiance. Two minutes before he was to pick me up, Jack called and merely said, "I'm not going" and hung up. I was crushed. Kathy said to come alone and when I got to the lake, there was Kent with his boat and a couple of guys. He invited me in his boat and tried to help me get over the disappointment of being stood up. I appreciated it and liked him a little more after that. We began going out every now and then and he'd tell me his girlfriend problems.

It seems they all wanted to marry him and he wanted to play the field until he was twenty-five. Since neither of us were interested in marriage (at least not to each other), we began having long, frank talks.

After breaking the waterskiing date, Jack stopped calling me. I was totally bewildered and brokenhearted. I decided he had started dating me to get my hopes up again so he could dump me and get even with me for divorcing him.

A couple long months of rejection dragged by. Out of sheer loneliness, I finally went out with the guy who had never ceased begging me to marry him and let him make love to me. Three more agonizing months went by, and I knew without a doubt I was pregnant. If I thought I had trouble before...I couldn't fathom how to cope with this one.

I was a basket case. I'd wake up in the morning and indescribable fear would come crashing in on me. Back then my little farming community did not tolerate illegitimate children. I was too ashamed to tell my parents. I was already looked down upon for having gotten a divorce. Not only that, they'd have forced me to marry the father, and that would have been my idea of hell on earth. I had no idea in the world what to do.

Just then a strange turn of events took place. I went out with Kent one night, and he told me he loved me and wanted to marry me! I was completely shocked and replied, "Kent, I have a terrible problem. If I ever figure out how to get through it and you're anywhere around, then we can talk about it, but not now."

He kept asking me for the next three weeks to tell him my problem. I was getting more pregnant and more desperate by the day. Finally, I confessed to him and he said, "Well, no problem. We'll get you an abortion."

He took me to a Catholic medical student friend of his who was going to perform it, but first he thought he ought to warn me of the possible harmful results. Remember, abortions were not legal then. He convinced me it would be safer and healthier to give birth to the baby. Not being Christians, Kent and I both thought of abortion as merely throwing away an egg but possibly bleeding to death or not being able to have more children really frightened me.

Kent said, "Well, we'll get married and place the baby for adoption. Pick a state you like, and we'll move there." I saw no other choice so I said, "Let's go to Colorado."

I knew I didn't love him but I had loved Jack and the marriage failed anyway so I figured I had nothing to lose.

I called Jack and asked to see him. He seemed glad to see me, and I asked him one more time to come back to me. He put his head down for a while and then, as he had done so many times before, pounded the steering wheel but said nothing. I thought, "Well, he doesn't want me un-pregnant, so he sure doesn't want me pregnant." It was December, and as I turned my face to the window so he wouldn't see my tears, Elvis Presley came on the radio singing, *"It'll Be A Blue, Blue Christmas Without You"*. I remember thinking sadly, "How true" and my insides hurting so bad I thought I would explode.

I never saw Jack again.

Kent and I were married soon after and, in Colorado, we found a Catholic Charity organization who agreed to help us find a good home for my baby. It is very painful for me to speak those words. I am still working hard at "forgetting the shame of my youth" as Isaiah 54 says. The sister assigned to my case took down all the information about our physical characteristics and ethnic backgrounds. Soon she'd found a couple in her file who had been waiting two years for a baby. She assured me they were lovely people.

I'll bet this nun was born-again because she really loved me and never judged me. I felt like a slut enough all by myself without any help from anyone else. I forced myself not to think of it as a real baby - my baby - because I could never bring it home and raise an illegitimate child with that stigma on it, and Kent would not accept it as his.

While Kent was out selling encyclopedias, I huddled in our basement apartment, this time alone in a strange city in a strange state till midnight or later. I was still afraid but we had bought a watchdog for me so I had it to cuddle. Sometimes I went along and read by flashlight in the car but a lot of time I sat alone contemplating my growing stomach and pining away over Jack. I hoped he'd never find out the shameful reason I begged him to marry me one minute and left town married to someone else the next.

I made a conscious decision to transfer every bit of loyalty I could muster to Kent and vowed to myself I would be a good wife to him for helping me through the roughest time of my life. I was grateful that he didn't seem to look down on me or condemn me. I began to totally depend on him for all my security.

I wrote to two close girlfriends who knew my situation. I'd always say, "I'm forgetting Jack. Kent is so good to me; I'm forgetting Jack". I hoped if I said it enough times, maybe it would happen, and I'd never even heard of Mark 11:24!

Kent was very good to me. We sort of ignored the pregnancy like it didn't exist. We bought an old "Snortin' Norton" motorcycle and explored all over Colorado.

During those months, I was hunting for God as hard as I knew how. Kent had been raised Lutheran. I thought maybe the Lutherans knew God so we joined a church, and I got confirmed a Lutheran. I did not find God there.

We lived in the basement apartment of an older couple's home. I'd hear the wife ranting and raving obscenities at her milk-toast husband. She would sneak into our apartment and read our mail. Once she held up our paycheck, and we ate applesauce for a week till we got it. I was so frightened of her we finally moved. However, she found out where we lived and I'd see her white Cadillac parked down the street and her spying on me. I was frantic, and I'd pull all the shades down, lock the doors and huddle in the dark til Kent came home. We soon found out why. She had completely misunderstood my letters and thought we were giving up our own baby. When it was born, she sent my parents a telegram telling them about it. The day I arrived home from the hospital, physically and emotionally drained, my parents called crying about the baby. I panicked and said, "What baby? I've told you before the landlady is crazy. She must be trying to stir up trouble."

They bought it so we got away with it.

I never had the nerve to let them know what a bad person I turned out to be - especially since they thought I had been doing bad things since I was fourteen. They had told me from then on that I was such a rebel I'd land in reform school. I never could figure out why they predicted that. The worst things any kids I knew did in those days were drink beer and steal hubcaps. They didn't go to reform school for that, and I never even did either of those things! But I had already ruined their reputation by the divorce, and I just couldn't face proving them right anymore. Since I couldn't stand to marry the father, it would've been needless pain for them, I felt, and the child would have had an emotional basket case for a mother.

I recovered very fast, and we returned to Iowa to start over. I comforted myself that the child had a better life than I ever could've given it under the circumstances. I felt I would break under any more guilt, so I put this one on the back burner and decided to make a success of my life from then on.

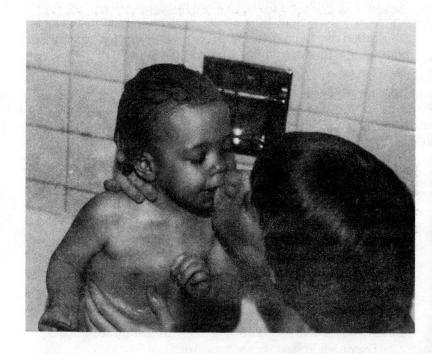

Kristin (12) bathing Mandy (1).

4

JESUS IS REAL

Soon after we had come home and fixed up a house, I thought my ordeal was over and we would settle down. I was wrong. Kent was offered a manager's position in an encyclopedia sales office in Indianapolis, a very high-paying job for a 21-year old. I pleaded not to move to a strange city again, but he wouldn't consider not going. He had put aside his career for me in Colorado. Now it was time for him to be successful.

He ran a crew of guys who would travel to different cities and sell. When he snapped his fingers, they jumped. He was very good at motivating, and he learned very early how to control people and keep them "psyched up."

He was rejected as a child by teachers who told him how stupid he was, saying "Why aren't you smart like your older brother who gets such good grades?"

He almost didn't make it through high school because they convinced him that he was so dumb. After that, he set out to prove himself and he got even with those teachers. He applied for a job in the paper that read, "You can make thousands of dollars a year. Be at our office on Monday.''

He got the job and was trained at nineteen and became a cracker-jack salesman. He was accomplishing his objective -- overcoming that rejection by making lots of money and wielding power.

Kent would come home from work at one or two o'clock in the morning, get up with bounding energy and be at his office again by nine a.m. Here I was once more alone in a strange city with no friends all day and into the night. Being alone til 8:00 or 9:00 in my home town was a picnic compared to this. The city was so big I didn't even know how to drive in it. That didn't matter much since Kent said he didn't want his wife working so I had nowhere to go anyway. Whatever he wanted was what I tried to do. But after earning my own money for three years, I felt like it was begging to ever ask for any money other than for groceries. When he was home on weekends, we entertained his sales crew which he felt was part of the success game. If they attained a certain sales goal which he set, we took them waterskiing or to nightclubs. Kent had gotten a key to the Chicago Playboy Club which, I must say, seemed to be quite a prestigious motivation for his guys. Sometimes he would suggest I get a new cocktail dress for one of these occasions. He would go along and decide if the dress was sharp enough and write out the check. Life in the fast lane had begun along with my total dependency on him.

I had one neighbor who was a spiritualist. Her dead grandma appeared regularly to her in her kitchen. So she taught me about spiritualism and reincarnation. I read to blind ladies in a nearby rest home, borrowed my other neighbor's English literature books from college to try to educate myself, and sewed clothes for several of my other girlfriend's kids back home trying to fight off the fear that would come over me at dusk.

There were so many crimes in Indianapolis the front page would always be plastered with the latest. I would pace the floor and cuddle my dog until Kent got home. I existed this way for over a year in constant fear every night that caused a knot in my stomach from being alone in a strange city.

One night at 3 a.m. I was at the window looking for Kent

to come home when I noticed my neighbor carrying her kids, running to the house next to hers. We were all aware of a rapist in the neighborhood lately. He had climbed in a window, knocked out the father, and raped the daughter. In fact, Kent had bought me a 38 and taught me to use it on account of this. This girl was running with her children next door because the intruder had been scratching on her screens. A few nights later, it happened to me! It was late at night and there was a loud, eery witch's laugh right at my open bedroom window. With shaking fingers, I forced myself to dial wondering all the while if I'd be shot while I dialed. I was too afraid to go shut the window and my dog was barking ferociously trying to force his way through the screen at whoever was out there. When my neighbor sleepily answered, I said, "Open your door; I've got to come over!"

Perhaps my dog scared the prowler because we made it next door safely.

When Kent finally got home, I told him what had happened and said, "I can't take this anymore. I'm going home."

I considered divorcing him because I hated this way of life but now I had this stigma of divorce on me and thought, "I just can't go around getting divorces. I've got to make this one work. I don't want everyone to think I'm completely unstable." I also felt I "owed him" for the favor he'd done for me by giving me a respectable reason to leave town. Otherwise, I don't believe I'd have stayed under such conditions. Our whole way of life was completely against my upbringing, and I was so lonely.

I told him, "You are such a good salesman. You can sell in Nebraska and Iowa as well as Indiana. Do what you want to do, but I'm afraid to stay alone here one more night."

He knew that I meant it. I couldn't take it anymore. I had to go home where all of my friends, relatives, and family were. If he had to stay out till three in the morning, at least I would have somewhere to go. He gave in, and sent me back to Iowa the next day. He came later with our furniture.

Even though Kent wasn't home much, at least we didn't fight, and I wasn't so lonely now that I had dear friends to

---

43

spend time with. He seemed to care about me when he was home, but when I tried to tell him how badly I craved more of a family life, he couldn't comprehend. We bought a piece of property, with virgin timber, and we were going to build a beautiful home on it. We would go there some weekends and cut dead limbs and clear the brush. Heaven knows that he made enough money to pay for a house, but he was building an empire so every time we got some spare money, he would buy a piece of property instead, and my dream home got put off. We owned houses and apartments, land, a laundry, and lived in a cracker box. We drove two Mercedes, but we couldn't pay the light bill on time. I had to pick out new carpeting for the apartments we owned, while the carpet in our own home was ugly and worn out. All of this frustrated me beyond words, but he had done this favor for me - rescued me in my fallen condition - so whatever he asked, that was what I did. I felt I owed it to him. I concentrated on designing a house on the land. It was all I looked forward to. I constantly read decorator books and had every room planned out. A gaping hole where we dug the basement is as far as we ever got.

The Vietnam War started and Kent was going to be drafted. The only thing that would keep him out was Kennedy's edict that expectant fathers were exempt. So we decided that I would get pregnant and keep him out of the war.

We had a darling little girl and named her Kristin. Life really took on meaning for me, and I devoted all my time to her. She became almost my whole reason for living. I loved being a mother, but now the guilt over giving my first child away overwhelmed me. At the time of the adoption I had no idea how much I could love my own child. I only knew then that I was an emotional wreck and was hardly able to handle a divorce let alone what people would say if I had a child with no father. But still I blamed myself for not being stronger. I began punishing myself for giving that baby away while I poured my life into Kristin. I did everything with her and for her. Now I was really locked into Kent because I had his baby, and I was sure I couldn't earn enough money to support her alone, although I still didn't like the way that he earned his living.

Being alone most of the time with a toddler got to me. An old boy friend came around and said to me, "It should have been you and me, babe. Let's have an affair."

I was beginning to be suspicious that Kent must have other women in other cities since he paid so little attention to me and never seemed to need sex. I thought about it and even though I knew it was wrong, I felt so unloved and lonely, a month later, I gave in.

That put me on a merry-go-round for six years of searching for another husband. Kent was almost never home, and I had found out for certain he had other women. I hated his way of life and felt I'd paid back my debt to him. I'd been true to him, but he had not been true to me, so I considered the debt cancelled. I went with a lot of guys from doctors to thieves and in between, trying to find the answer to life and who or what was going to make me happy. Part of me hoped that I would never find the ideal guy who would make me leave Kent because I remembered the trauma when my parents almost split up. I kept thinking, "As miserable as I am, I just cannot do that to my daughter. I don't want Kristin to grow up without her father."

During this time Kent admitted he had been having affairs from the beginning of our marriage and we began having what one author called an "open marriage". We decided that being honest about it was much better than being deceitful.

Knowing that we looked very successful but owed all over town only added to my frustrations. I was sure people would look down on us if they knew. From time to time, friends happened to be around when a collection agent came and they would say they didn't see how I could stand to live that way.

My parents made comments on my being alone so much. I always stuck up for Kent but inside, I secretly agreed with them. Dad never made much money but he paid his bills on time and everyone knew his word was as good as gold. I longed to have that kind of reputation.

Except for my daughter, my life for the most part had become loneliness and disappointment. When Kent came home every couple of weeks, we would party all weekend because it had become too miserable to be alone together.

Then it happened. Kent met a girl who swept him off his feet, and he wanted to marry her. So after throwing me a wing-ding of a surprise birthday party, he left me and filed for divorce. The realization that my whole life was a shambles came crashing in on me. I was sick of my adultery. I was sick of everything. The fear of poverty came on me like a ton of bricks.

After three days of non-stop crying and no sleep, I called a couple that we used to nightclub with, Lee and Carolyn Huelle. She had been a professional singer, and I used to worry that they drank too much. A year before they had found Christ as their Saviour and quit drinking. Lee had sold encyclopedias for a rival company and that was how he and Kent met. Now they both sold siding for houses together in the same company. I wound up on their door step thinking that he would know where I could find Kent because I sure didn't.

I was a wreck. I had always managed to be the life of the party on the outside, and now I hadn't been able to quit crying for three days. Before I got to her house, Carolyn got down on her knees and prayed, "Lord, Dru has shut me up every time I have tried to talk to her about You. If You don't give me an opening, I'm not going to say anything to her."

I got there and she made me a cup of tea. I remember I couldn't stop tears from running down my face into the teacup. Her sister had been miraculously healed of cancer and she had told me all about it. So I said to her, "Carolyn, I know that your church believes in physical healing... can they do anything for emotional problems?"

I actually looked around to see what dummy said that because I was practically atheistic by that time. I ran around with a bunch of humanistic people, I didn't seem to have any prayers answered, and I couldn't figure the Bible out. Years before I had left Jesus behind somewhere as a myth or a historical character. She clapped her hands and said, "Dru, that's our specialty!"

Just then, Lee, who had gone to work, suddenly appeared in the door with three different kinds of Bibles. They talked to me all day. I asked them every theological question about God that all the preachers couldn't answer for me as a child. They weren't too old in the Lord, and they weren't prepared for all of my intellectual questions. I never noticed that after I asked a question, one of them was always out of the room for a while. Then pretty soon that one would come back into the room carrying a Bible, saying, "God's Word says right here..." and would give me the answer to my question.

Later they told me that when I asked a question and they didn't know the answer, one would go to the other room and call their pastor, and he would give them the Scripture reference while the other kept me busy talking. The one on the phone would return to the room and give me the pastor's answer. I thought they were walking Bibles!

That night they took me with them to Glad Tidings in Omaha. I saw all of these happy people, and I knew that they were not high on anything. I could tell that they had something that I didn't have. They were praying for a lady who was supposed to have major surgery, and I thought, "At least I'm not as bad off as her. I don't have to have knives cut into me. I should be thankful for that."

She turned around (they had all laid hands on her); she was glowing! I thought, "What have these people got?"

Pastor Walker agreed to counsel me, and I wasn't even a member of his church! I was amazed at the love shown me. That night when we returned to their house, I said, "I give up. I want what you've got. But I don't believe in this Jesus business. I don't know what it meant when He died on the cross and all of that stuff."

Lee said, "That's okay, Dru. Tell Him you don't believe in Him. But ask Him to come into your heart and manifest Himself to you anyway."

Carolyn had never heard of anyone being led to the Lord that way, and she thought, "Oh no! What is he doing? That won't work!" but she sat there serenely smiling and didn't say a word of what she feared.

I was so far from God at that time that if they had said to pray to the television set, it would have been easier. I can

Kristin and me in front of our window the
first Christmas after we were born-again.

Kristin, 11, holding little Mandy she prayed for,
6 months.

remember some counselor that I had gone to for transactional analysis trying to get me to pound on the chair to take out my anxieties and frustrations. I informed him that I could not do such a silly thing since that chair had never done anything to me in its life. I had paid good money to have psychologists tell me to do strange sounding things so if Lee and Carolyn wanted me to pray in the air, then I would pray in the air. What did I have to lose?

So I said, "Lord, if You are really there" (giving myself an out), "come and do something worthwhile with my life. I've messed it up so bad, but if You're really there, You can take it and do whatever You want with me."

I guess I expected thunder or lightning so after a few seconds, I said, "Well, nothing happened."

Carolyn is saying to herself, "I knew it, Lee blew it. I never heard a prayer like that."

But Lee said, "It will."

On the way out to the kitchen to make some ice tea, I started to say a swear word but my throat choked up, and I couldn't get it out. It scared me. I thought I was psyched up or something so I decided I wouldn't tell them. Instead, I heard myself say, "I can't swear!" Then as I opened the refrigerator door, all of a sudden anger, hatred, fear, bitterness, and resentment came up from inside of me and left! I felt it go and a real supernatural love started coming in from the other side. I knew that it didn't matter what Kent had ever done; I forgave him. At the same time, after three days of heart palpitations that kept me awake all night, I felt my heart slow down to normal, and the tears stopped! I stood there feeling clean and innocent as a child. I started giggling, saying, "Jesus is real! Jesus is real!"

5
A DOORMAT

"Wow, if Kent could get Jesus, we would have it made!" I exclaimed to Lee and Carolyn.

"That's what we've been trying to tell you all day," they answered.

The three of us prayed that Kent would be born again, changed, and come home.

I went so gung ho for God that I read my Bible almost day and night. Kent wanted me to come sign for the divorce and get a job all in one day. I went to the lawyer's office and said, "This is not going to happen." I signed the papers anyway as there was a three-month waiting period.

I asked Lee how I would know the right job to take. Having to go to work after eleven and a half years at home was scary. He said, "You will feel a peace on the inside about the right job."

I had a lot of job interviews, and at each one I felt sick inside. Then my girlfriend, Reta, offered me a job in her beauty salon. She could only pay me minimum-wage, but I felt terrific about it. I analyzed hair under a microscope, mixed shampoo, cleaned the place, sold products, and led people to the Lord while they were getting their hair shampooed. I had a wonderful time. She was raised a Baptist but had backslidden by that time. All of her Baptist friends would come in her salon, and she would tell them, "Dru is a new Christian. She just got born again."

Some would smile and whisper, "Don't get mixed up with those tongue talkers."

I was already going to church with a bunch of enthusiastic charismatics who would shout, "Hey, Dru is born again! Look, we have a new Christian!"

Whoever they told would yell back, "Hallelujah!"

I didn't understand the quiet Baptists, and I was already a tongue-talker.

I really enjoyed that job. Kent would come in and buy cosmetics for his girlfriend just to show me that he was not coming home. The girls in the beauty shop were absolutely dumbfounded. How could I be so nice to this rotten guy? I was so ecstatic to have found out Jesus was for real that nothing else mattered. I wound up leading every girl I worked with to the Lord. Reta re-dedicated her life and became a... you guessed it... a tongue talker!

I was learning to operate in love in spite of everything that Kent could think up to do. I continued to thank God that he would be born-again, changed, and come home. Knowing Jesus really existed and I was going to heaven when I died made my problems with Kent pale in comparison.

A month later he came to Lee's house one night to pick up our daughter. We had been to a week-long evangelistic meeting, and I had seen a couple of miraculous healings. I was bubbling over with the joy of the Lord. Kent had taken his girlfriend out to Las Vegas and Disney Land where the world is supposed to have so much fun, and he could see that we had had a better time in church back in Omaha! He started weeping and gave his heart to the Lord that night. We sang hymns until one o'clock in the morning. I thought he was going to come home, but he didn't. Instead, he left to get his girlfriend born-again! He had decided without God in their lives they couldn't possibly make it. I was stunned and said,

"God! What's happening?"

The Lord then impressed me to pray for her to be born-again because, He said, "She needs Me, too."

That was to be another exercise in walking in love. Kent started bringing his girlfriend to our church. They would sit towards the front, and I would sit in the back with Lee and Carolyn. Our seven-year-old daughter, Kristin, would go up and sit with them a while, and then she would come back and sit with me. After two weeks of this, on a Sunday night, I had my head bowed during the altar call and Carolyn's sister poked me and said, "Look, look who just ran down to the altar."

Kent's girlfriend gave her heart to the Lord. She began reading the Bible and found out that divorce wasn't in God's original plan.

So Kent told her of a Scripture that he had heard recently that said, "Old things are passed away, all things are new. Dru's and my marriage was my old life." When we told our testimony, I used to say, "But this 'old thing' hadn't passed away yet."

I really got into the faith message. I was confessing to anyone who asked, "My marriage is healed; my husband is coming home; and everything is hunky-dory."

The night that Kent got born again he made a pact with God and said, "I give You my will God, but I don't want to go back to Dru. If You speak to me telling me to go back to her I will, but I'm not going to go back just because a bunch of Christians hit me over the head with their Bibles."

He began going to Bible studies and noticed a couple who seemed to be very knowledgeable about the Scriptures. He asked them if he could go home with them one night after Bible study and talk. He asked them all kinds of questions about divorce. No matter what he asked, he just couldn't get it out of them that God took it lightly. They were crying with compassion over how miserable we were together. They read the Bible to him and really didn't try to counsel out of their heads. Finally, Kent stretched out on the floor and heard the words, "It's Me."

He got up off of the floor, called me in Council Bluffs at

11:30 P.M., and said, "I'm coming home. Your prayers are answered."

I asked him, "Are you sure that you want to?"

"No, I don't want to, but God has spoken to me," was his reply.

That was not exactly the answer that I had hoped for, but I ran out of the house in my nightgown to the neighbors across the street telling them that Kent was coming home.

I felt sure that Jesus was going to shake His magic wand over Kent and turn him into my prince charming. There were so many areas between us that needed healing, but I had blind faith that God was going to fix them all because He wanted families to stay together.

I wanted Kent changed, or I knew that it wasn't going to work. I was working on anything that I felt needed changing in me just as hard as I could. If God had told me to paint myself purple and bay at the moon, I would have done it. "- Just anything You say, Lord."

I needed Kent to want to be home, to be a good father and a good husband. I desired him to stop borrowing money, to stop spending more than we made, and to pay the bills on time. Of course, I wanted to love him and him to love me so that we had no need of outside affairs. I was sick and tired of that lifestyle. I craved a real home life - not just for me but for Kristin too.

A lot of people have asked me, "What was it like when he walked in the door?"

They pictured me coming down the stairs in a flimsy negligee, running into his arms romantically kissing. That was not the way it was. We embraced very soberly and we didn't kiss. It was a real scary hug because we both knew that we did not love each other. We were doing this only because we felt God wanted us to. We knew that we had a long, hard road ahead of us.

We were now both in love with Jesus if not in love with each other. We would sit down and pray in tongues for hours at a time. Kent was his own boss so he didn't have to go to work if he didn't want to. We hit every meeting, every Bible study, and we read the Bible alone and together. We found out that God wasn't big on strife so we decided not to yell at one another, and we talked everything over as best we could. We tried to come to a mutual agreement on things. Kent wanted to be as happy as I wanted to be. So we would talk things over and pray in the Spirit for hours and try to yield to one another. We tried to be very unselfish.

When I was praying Kent home, I had said to myself, "When he walks in that door, I will have to do what he wants. I will have to toe the mark or he probably won't stay home."

I had been quite a women's libber, and I now thought that was anti-God, so I was ready to turn myself into a doormat if necessary. One of the first Christian books I read was on wives submitting to their husbands no matter what. Now I thought I had a Scriptural backup to do what I knew I had to do to keep him home...I could "submit as unto the Lord."

So with my being in this frame of mind, we reached agreement on issues pretty easily.

The story got out about our miraculous reconciliation. Glad Tidings was a big church. Everybody had watched Kent bring his girlfriend to church and then watched us get back together. They saw us come diligently to church every service and sing in the choir. It wasn't long before Women's Aglow and other organizations began asking me to give my testimony. I really wanted to serve God even though I was terrified to get up on the stage in front of people. But for God I managed to do it. Kent would always go along and introduce me and help me get going. Then once I got into my story, I'd stop feeling nervous, and I'd tell him, "You can sit down now; I'm fine," and everybody would laugh.

Everyone who heard of us began sending people to our house who had marriage problems. We were baby Christians, and yet we were counseling Christians much older in the Lord with marriage problems. A lot of halves of couples came to find out how to pray their partners home. Since I had taken faith teachings and Scriptures on physical healing and translated them into marriage healing, I thought everyone else could do it too so I told them they could get their marriage healed by faith the same way that a person gets his body healed by faith.

I taught them how to pray in faith and believe they would receive when they prayed. I gave them quotes from the Scriptures on Godly characteristics, told them to begin confessing that was what their husband or wife was like, and encouraged them to act in love no matter what their partner did to them.

Last of all according to Ephesians 6:13, I advised them "...having done all [the crisis demands], to stand [firmly in your place]." (Amplified)

Consequently, groups began springing up all over the country, and they called themselves "Standers."

As the groups began to multiply, they would ask us to come and speak. We would travel to designated cities every month and speak to the "Standers." Kent did most of this traveling for the first few years because we couldn't afford for both of us to travel, and he thrived on speaking in front of people. On the other hand, it was hard for me so I figured he was the preacher in the family.

We were asked to hold a marriage seminar in Ft. Collins, Colorado. In preparation for the seminar I typed up everything that I could think of on how to pray your spouse home. I put it in a pamphlet with a bright yellow cover called, "AND THEY SHALL BE ONE FLESH." We distributed it to the people that came to the marriage seminar in Ft. Collins. Little did we dream how many people in that seminar would send my pamphlets from coast to coast, to every friend they knew whose husband or wife had left them. We began getting letters from people all over the United States asking, "Can we have ten copies of THE YELLOW BOOK?"

"Here's money for twenty-five yellow books."

Many people began asking, "Can we be involved?

The "Stander" groups used my yellow book as their curriculum along with the Bible and other faith books. We became "marriage experts" over night, and a ministry was born.

During the early days of the ministry a couple came for help. They were fighting like cats and dogs. I didn't even know that they were Christians because of the language that came out of their mouths. After listening to them scream at each other for a while, I asked, "Have you ever heard of being born again?"

"Are you kidding?" they blustered. "We have been saved since... I'm a deacon in the church... she's a Sunday School teacher..., etc." were their answers.

They were insulted that I asked such a question. When I found out that they had both had the born again experience, in an attempt to get through to them, I said, "Then, you can have a born-again marriage!"

The name of the ministry came out of that counseling session.

I wanted to serve God with all of my heart and thought that surely He must be behind all of this.

Respect for Kent began to return when I saw him wanting to serve God. He also cleaned out the bill drawer, quit spending, sold everything, and we did not have to file bankruptcy. My faith level was "sky high" and we were doing our best to operate in the God-kind of unconditional love with each other. I felt sure God would cause us to fall all the way in love.

I had such a zeal to see homes healed, to help as many little kids from hurting like I had hurt when my parents nearly broke up.

All the healing between Kent and me that I had prayed for had not happened yet, but here we were on stage in the public eye. People with broken homes and couples in trouble flocked to our meetings. They were thrilled that God had brought us back together. We were their in-the-flesh example of what they hoped God would do for them. Everywhere we went, we were received with much love. They all thought we were a perfect couple so I began to not want to disappoint all of them just as much as I wanted happiness for myself.

Sometimes we'd end a seminar with questions from the audience. Being optimistic by nature, I concentrated all my thoughts on the good parts of our marriage and it wasn't too difficult for me to speak my faith desire on areas in our marriage that really weren't healed yet. But I used to pray that no one would ask us anything about sex. That part of our marriage was so lacking for me that I was afraid to even mention it to Kent for fear he would be hurt by my attitude. I just kept praying about it secretly to God, and I think even Kent thought my "faith" statements expressed how I really felt.

I don't think now that I handled it right at all, but here we were considered the "counselors" so I felt I couldn't go to a counselor. I was afraid to hurt Kent's feelings, and I was brainwashed by my understanding of the faith message (that I must speak what I wanted and not what I really had or I'd never get what I wanted.) And I sure couldn't say to hundreds of people who came to our seminars thinking we had it all together, "Listen, our sex life really stinks, but let me tell you about agreement. We can really tell you how to come to agreement on difficult situations, but let's not discuss sex."

Instead, I quoted some advice I'd read out of a favorite Christian book on sex. It was such a dilemma to be smiling blissfully on the outside for all the people but be in acute pain on the inside whenever the subject came up. As the years went by, I tried harder and harder to do what the faith message said; that is, DO what you are supposed to do and the feelings will follow. Never, never go by your feelings.

When Kent first came home, I used to stay up late reading the Bible and sneak into the bed to avoid having sex. Then I read the verse in the Scripture that says to withhold sex from your partner is to defraud them. So for Jesus, I quit going to bed after Kent had fallen asleep. I even tried to work up a little creativity, but unfortunately for me, I am a romantic and manufacturing sex for the sake of obedience seemed phony to me.

I had read the Song of Solomon so I knew God created romance and the "eros" or passionate kind of love and wanted it in marriage. I used to cry out to God, "This is crazy! I know You are going to fix this because You've given us a marriage ministry. We are really living everything else we are teaching. Father, I might think this is my cross that I have to bear, but if You have called me to be a marriage teacher, surely You don't want me to go on forever teaching something I'm not living."

I always read everything on sex in every Christian marriage book I could get my hands on. They all said it was good;

everyone should like it; here are all these ways to do it. But none seemed to know the secret of how to put "eros" love in a marriage if it wasn't already there so that making love would be the joyous, spontaneous experience I read about in the Song of Solomon.

Let me make it very clear that Kent certainly was in no way at fault. If he had asked me what he could do better, I wouldn't have been able to think of anything, which was another reason I didn't know how to talk to him about it. The only thing I could have said was that the "magic" just wasn't there. Also there was so much teaching against giving ground to feelings that I half wondered if there was something wrong with me for having any.

The only reason I write about it now is I've come to see it as no insult to Kent but rather an indictment against me for marrying out of desperation instead of love and all the other meaningful reasons.

Unfortunately for both Kent and me, we had experienced "eros" in other relationships so I'm sure he missed it as much as I did. In fact, he used to scold me for not being more passionate but, I swear before God, I did as well as I could do. I still don't know the secret. If I did, I'm sure I could make a fortune writing "how to" books.

Except for that area of our life, I was happier than I had been in years and years. I was serving God and helping people. Marriages were being healed as a result of our testimony. Best of all, people were getting born-again by praying the prayer I'd written in my yellow book. I rationalized that, after all, sex was only a few minutes of my life so I would just have to tolerate it and look upon the marriage healings as my reward for staying together.

Soon after our reconciliation, Kent began to get "messages from the Lord" when we would sit down and pray. He would say, "Get a pencil," and I would take them down in shorthand.

If I ever had a hard time coming to agreement with what Kent wanted, he'd always get a message that set me straight, and I would end up apologizing or agreeing with him. They didn't start out that way, but after I began to believe wholeheartedly these messages were from God, that was the tone they took. This was how we reached the "heartfelt agreement" we taught at all our meetings.

One message said that my fulfillment in life would only come from fulfilling Kent's every desire. That was the purpose of a wife's existence and the only way I could ever be happy. Naturally I wanted to be happy so I truly tried to meet his every wish whenever we were together and taught this wherever I spoke. (I always got a lot of amens from the husbands.)

I could have my hands in three cooking pots at one time, but if he called for iced tea from the living room, I dropped everything and brought it to him.

Once a dinner guest disgustedly remarked, "Are his legs broken? Here, let me stir the gravy while you take the lord and master his tea."

I thought to myself, "This dear person just doesn't understand the role of a submissive wife."

I did not resent this. I thought this was what God wanted me to do. Only recently have people who were guests in our home opened up and told me that they went away saying, "If that's how they expect us to live, with her jumping when he wants something - forget it."

If a couple wanted us to pray with them, Kent got a message right away and... case closed. It was only recently people opened up to me and said they didn't buy this "message" business when we prayed with them. I was shocked. I thought we were being the model Christian couple. If I ever got thoughts that I was being "put upon" or used, I thought it was the devil and I lectured myself about being more dedicated in my submission.

Another message said that we were not to go to counselors or anyone with our problems. We were called to this marriage ministry, and we should sit down and pray together and God Himself would give us the answers. Thus, a trap of blind submission was set for me because if I ever objected to the messages, I was in disobedience and out of the will of God. I never personally received messages like that so I had no confidence in myself to dare question them. I really thought it was God, but I did wonder why I was the one who always had the shaping up to do. Sometimes I got discouraged when told to improve in my submission. I was trying harder than any other woman I knew but it was never good enough.

After we were saved about three years, I seemed to be having pregnancy symptoms. The most alarming thing was I couldn't remember how that could possibly be. Then it crept into my mind, "Oh, yes. There was a time about three months ago."

You see, it took me until after Mandy was born to submit to the Scripture verse about not defrauding your spouse sexually.

I was thrilled because I wanted to have more than one child in our family. When our marriage was in trouble, I didn't think that I could handle another child. I had the full responsibility of Kristin because Kent was on the road all of the time. We had another darling little girl named Mandy Carolee. Her middle name was after Lee and Carolyn who led me to the Lord.

Again I had most of the responsibility because now Kent was on the road for the Lord. Thoughts plagued me that he had merely traded his briefcase for a Bible, but I tried to fight them off.

After her birth, I was stricken with such a loss of energy that I almost couldn't make it through the day. I felt like I was on my death bed. I went to doctors, but they couldn't find a thing wrong with me. I suppose now, as I look back on it all, it was stress. I use to drag myself onto airplanes to do meetings. I would be in my best clothes, lying flat on the floor of some pastor's study while Kent and he discussed preliminaries of the meeting. Then somebody would help me struggle to my feet, and I would walk dizzily out onto the stage and trust God to help me stay on my chair while I ministered. When the meeting was over, I would collapse backstage, my heart racing so frantically I couldn't get the rest my body seemed to crave. Everybody wants to take you out to dinner after you have done a meeting. I didn't have the strength to sit at the table so I hardly ever went along.

I would go back to my room weeping in exhaustion and fear that I was dying in my mid-thirties and my kids would grow up without a mother. I searched my heart and could find no sin, and I was following all the submission and faith rules. I would reason with God, "I have a healing covenant with You, and I can't serve You if I die early."

At times I was almost overwhelmed struggling to be a fulltime wife, mother, and traveling minister. I never had any privacy or time to rest. On the road I was in front of people and at home, ministry workers were in and out all day as the ministry operated out of our basement. The constant call of "mother and minister" tugged me in different directions with no let up. It never occurred to me to ask for a rest or help. I did tell Kent once that I feared I was going to land in the hospital. He couldn't comprehend how desperate I felt. He'd say, "Oh, you'll make it," and off he'd go to minister to other wives whose husbands had left them. I tried not to resent his running off to meet their needs while ignoring mine. My body and nerves felt as though I was going to pieces. When he left like clock-work every other week, I feared I couldn't handle even Mandy's needs because I got to the place where I could hardly function. Kent wouldn't stay home because he feared the offerings would quit and the ministry would shut down. I tried to fight off thoughts that he only needed me to keep the ministry going. After all, I too, wanted to serve God so I understood his compulsion to keep going under all circumstances. I thought I had to keep going too. I thought if I quit doing meetings and rested, the ministry would suffer and it would be my fault. I did not want to fail God or all the people who depended on us.

6

MESSAGES FROM GOD

When the father of my first child got born again, I was very glad, but I was not quite prepared when he and his wife began attending our church. And I certainly wasn't prepared for them to ask Kent and me to teach them how to pray.

Kent enjoyed being a teacher in any situation and agreed to do it even though he knew the role this man had played in my life. I was still under such a heavy guilt complex about giving the baby away and never telling him about it so, even though it was a bit bizarre, I reasoned that the Lord must be giving me an opportunity to make it all up to him spiritually. I thought we could pass on whatever we had learned from God and help him go through the baby Christian stage.

I was ready to do any foolish sounding thing for God. As it turned out, even though I thought it was God, in reality, it was only foolish!

"If it sounds crazy, it must be God" is not wise theology.

They came to our house often to pray with us. He and Kent were much alike. They were visionaries and would spend time dreaming up great projects to do for the Lord.

Soon both of them were getting "messages from the Lord." I would take these messages down in shorthand and between the two of them, I had soon filled a book.

The messages instructed the four of us to form a covenant and said that we were going to build a giant corporation that would funnel huge profits into the Kingdom of God. It all sounded very noble.

The four of us would pray for hours and hours while I kept my little toddler, Mandy, quiet. After they left, I'd collapse and cry from weariness. This was during my "energy crisis," and praying in the Spirit and keeping her silently entertained for hours so she would not disturb these solemn spiritual "summit meetings" wore my body and nerves to a frazzle.

A dear lady preacher friend of mine tried to tell me that "all Spirit and no Word" was not good, but it didn't sink in because I was convinced that God wanted us to do this.

I realize now I was in emotional bondage because of my guilt, and it caused me to lose all common sense.

Then, too, my unbearable fatigue forced me to concentrate all my energy on just surviving each day's demands. I had knowledge that personal "words from God" should agree with the Scriptures or be backed up by two or three witnesses, but it all slipped by me in the confusion. Besides, my husband was sure that we had been chosen to carry out this "special mission" for God and my whole duty was to submit to him.

One day this couple said, "We are anointed in business and you are anointed in ministry, so why don't you let us take over your business and run it for you? You can go into the ministry full time, and we'll all live off the business."

Kent was just champing at the bit to go into full-time ministry so he readily agreed.

Here the four of us were in such deception. The Bible

says in I Timothy 3:6 that a novice should not be given great things to do lest he be lifted up in pride. Actually all four of us were wet behind the ears as Christians. Kent and I had no theological training, just what we got at meetings and on tapes. We asked no one if what we were teaching agreed with the Scriptures. We just went out and taught our experience. We hadn't proved ourselves as beyond reproach, as I Timothy 3 goes on to say, and weren't taking good care of our families in the financial area. Yet we thought God had picked us to carry out this great special project.

As a person who dislikes confrontation and quarreling, submitting to my husband in all things sort of fit my personality. That doctrine plus my overwhelming guilt relating to the father of my first child were such levers over me, I could be talked into almost anything.

I marvel that I didn't put two and two together sooner. If this couple was so "anointed in business," why were they broke because each of their businesses had failed? They had reasons... someone else was always at fault.

They were broke and in debt; we were broke and in debt. I thought it might be nice if we went to work and paid off all the debts and gained trustworthy names in the marketplace, but that did not seem plausible to the other covenant members. We were on too "special" a mission to go to work for ordinary wages. I begged them to see that ordinary wages that paid the rent were a lot better than sitting around praying and getting no wages at all but my pleas fell on deaf ears.

You see, one of the articles of the covenant was that all four of us had to be in agreement before we made a move. I imagine I was looked upon as sort of a millstone around their neck that had to be tolerated. I was the only one of the four who felt the way I did, and they had to spend time convincing me to go their way.

We put all of our bills together. If money came in and they had a greater need than we did, even though we had earned the money or vice versa, the money would go to meet the more urgent need.

Their spirit and character changed after we obligated ourselves to this covenant. They became domineering and manipulative, trying to take control of every move. If I got a birthday present of $25, they would debate if I should split it!

The incredible insanity of it caused me to begin to suspect I was a pawn, but I was afraid God would be displeased with me if I did anything sinful like stand up to Kent. Instead, I cried out to God that if I wasn't crazy to think something was terribly wrong to get me out of this.

At the same time, the "Standers" groups were multiplying all over the country and we were receiving more and more requests to come and speak.

We got into a pyramid dry milk company. Kent began traveling around doing "milk meetings," and he would do a meeting for a "Standers" group in the same city. The milk business supplied his ticket and groceries for our two families but did not supply rent or any other living expenses for two couples and four children. Kent enjoyed promoting the business, but most people he talked to did not have time enough to make it profitable for themselves and, consequently, for us.

However, the "Standers" groups flourished with the regular pep talks. I told myself the healed marriages that resulted were worth my husband's being gone when I so desperately needed him.

Kent did not live inside my body and did not seem able to comprehend when I tried to tell him I did not feel physically able to be alone. He was exuberantly healthy. I think he thought I exaggerated when I tried to explain I felt faint when I walked across a room or too dizzy to intelligently cope with all the ministry decisions I had to make when he was gone. There was never any time to "let down" and rest with ministry volunteers going through my house all day long. When Kent was home, the covenant had to pray for hours. There was never any privacy or time to relax and enjoy being a family. Ministry calls came at all hours of the day and night. Kent never took the phone off the hook except to pray. My head began to ache so badly I'd look in the mirror to see if my eyes were really bulging out of my head or if it only felt that way. No pain killer helped. I began to fear I must have a brain tumor. I confessed healing and strength Scriptures and hung on to them.

Sometime I'd be so weak and in pain that in order to get to a meeting, I'd manage to dress. Then I'd order breakfast from room service and dial our intercessor. I'd hold the phone with one hand and eat with the other while she prayed for me and quoted healing Scriptures until I got the strength to leave the room and go minister.

I began to scream at Kristin if she didn't help me just right with Mandy or the house. Actually, she was the only one I wasn't in "submission" to so I realize now that I took out my frustrations on her. I didn't see this until I got my health back years later. I then asked her forgiveness. It's a miracle my relationship with her wasn't permanently jeopardized.

I began to loathe my life, and then I had to fight off the guilt that came from loathing the life I thought God had picked out for me!

The covenant couple did not know how to run our siding company. It became obvious that if Kent did not continue to sell, hire salesmen and installers, and run the jobs, the company was going to fold instead of supporting two families. Kent's mind and energies were on the ministry so eventually our business went broke, leaving us owing the I.R.S. thousands of dollars.

This couple was buying a farm which they rented out to make the payments. When the rent money came, they paid off covenant debts that accumulated because no one was working instead of using it to make the farm payments. They lost the farm eventually and wondered why. After all, we had a message saying God was going to save the farm.

When Mandy was a toddler, we discovered that due to inflation, we had enough equity to move into a much larger house in a quiet neighborhood I'd always loved.

The basement of this home housed the ministry. Now after months of praying and not working, our house that I loved dearly was dangerously close to foreclosure. I tried desperately to make the three of them see that you can't pray for a good garden without a hoe in your hand. I got down on my knees and showed Kent the Scriptures that say if you don't work, you don't eat and that a man who doesn't take care of his family is worse than an infidel. I would tell him that if I weren't so sick, I would go to work and pump gas or anything and beg him to go to work and not lose our house.

He would just say praying was his work and God was going to save our house. That's fine IF you have a personal revelation from God and God IS supplying your needs. But this wasn't revelation; it was deception.

In desperation, I watched our house go right down into foreclosure, and the three of them just sat around leisurely and prayed. I'd pace the floor at night asking God what was wrong and telling the devil he was not going to put my children and me out on the street. My life became a nightmare I could not wake up from. This couldn't really be happening, could it? Were they all crazy, or was I?

The sheriff became a regular visitor at our door delivering notices that he was to either get payments or confiscate our furniture or vehicles. Kent would stall him off and go sell something. This always made me feel like the scum of the earth, but it never bothered the other three. This was part of "suffering for Christ" when you have a "special mission for God" that no one else understands. Their attitude was the bill collectors were the bad guys, not us. I never could cope with that attitude. The Bible says the borrower is servant to the lender.

One day a lady who had been helped by our ministry called Kent to say she was getting an inheritance and didn't know what she should do with it. Since the ministry operated out of our basement, Kent asked her if she'd like to buy our house and become the ministry's landlady. She agreed. Kent went to the finance company and told them, and they cooperated by not publishing the foreclosure. Thus, we became renters and were supposed to buy it back from her in a year.

Kent said, "See, God has saved our house."

I was so frustrated. I knew that God had, but He shouldn't have had to!! We went from owner to renter. The time stretched from one into five years. When we finally bought it back, higher interest and other complications literally doubled the payments! What a waste of God's money.

Husbands take heed: A woman has an innate need for security. To a wife and mother, a home is not just a place to hang her hat. It is protection and shelter from the storms of life for her and her children. To threaten a wife with losing her home puts more stress on her than she was created to handle. Forget the women's libbers, guys. We still need you to protect us, and we still want to work outside the home by choice, not for survival. Spending precious time with your kids is a far more valuable investment than being able to give them all kinds of material possessions.

Recently in a Christian bookstore, I came across an excellent book by Dr. Kevin Leman called *The Pleasers - Women Who Can't Say No and the Men Who Control Them*. I discovered a lot about myself in that book.

A controller is someone who needs to feel important by running other people's lives. If things go wrong, it is always someone else's fault. I thought I was being submissive but in reality, I was just an "enabler" for three controlling spirits.

If someone is making you jump through hoops and you are enabling them to have a scapegoat for their failures year after year, I suggest you read this book. An enabler thinks he is being kind, loving, and forgiving, but they are actually enabling the controller to avoid facing reality and admitting his faults. Abused wives are enablers. Controllers will never submit to counseling as long as someone helps them keep their little game going. Why should they?

For those of us who have been enablers, to seek freedom forces us to walk into unknown territory. Our present life may be painful but at least we are familiar with the pain.

This is where I believe I was in the covenant and other areas of my life. I would rather suffer silently and avoid conflict. I didn't think I could cope with what might happen if I ever stood up to Kent and refused to back down from what I felt was right. At times I felt almost anything would be better than the financial pressure of our way of life but it was all I had and my only identity. I believe now the headaches and loss of energy stemmed from the horrible insecurity I lived in.

One message said our family was going to buy a bus and travel for the ministry the rest of our lives so we should give our beloved pets away. That caused me almost to faint.

Another day we got a "word" that we were to go that afternoon to a certain banker who would give us a loan. Off we went, and the banker promptly told us we were crazy in no uncertain terms. I said to Kent, "Isn't this proof to you that this message is not from the Lord and probably the others aren't either?" He said he didn't want to talk about it because he might become afraid to ever operate in the gifts of the Spirit.

A fellow Christian in Nebraska had gotten into the milk business and decided he didn't want to actively work it. He knew what a promoter Kent was so he invested $20,000 into our milk business. "Glory to God! We have money to live on!" said the covenant members. I said, "No, he expects that money to go into the milk business and be paid back with a share of the profits. This man invested his money in good faith; he trusts us. He didn't say to go buy clothes and pay our utility bills with it."

They replied, "You're wrong. This is God supplying our needs. God said to let this be one business that is not run out of need, and we have needs so we are going to use this money." They sat back, folded their arms, and glared at me for having the audacity to hold up the workings of the covenant. I was so convinced they were wrong that I actually held them off for a few days. But they finally wore me down and in sheer exhaustion, I gave in and told them to do what they wanted.

If I had been free to counsel with any logical-thinking people, they would've blown this covenant wide open for the deception it was. One message told us we didn't need to go to church. How deceived could we get? That was so obviously contrary to Scripture. I will never again isolate myself from the Christian body. Isolation and thinking you have a "special mission" from God that no one else understands opens you up to deception.

The covenant took all the $20,000 and spent it on our debts. The man was killed in a plane crash soon after, and his widow really needed the money. I really felt bad about this.

Early in my Christian walk, I had read a statement in one of Gloria Copeland's books, "You can't afford the luxury of strife." That is a very good teaching, but I took it too far and believed if I stood my ground for what I believed in and it caused an argument, I would be in strife so I always gave in. I also felt inferior because I didn't have energy like normal people.

Thank God, we had kept our ministry out of the covenant. Any money that was sent in for books and tapes was spent for printing books and tapes. It was run honestly, and I was proud of it even though it was small and operated out of our basement. I lived for the letters that came to us reporting marriage healings and salvations from praying the prayer I'd written in the yellow book.

One day after about two years in this covenant, Kent and I got off the plane from a ministry trip. We were supposed to go somewhere right away, but the covenant couple phoned the minute we walked in the door and called a prayer meeting. Already exhausted from the trip, nevertheless we hurried to see what urgent thing needed prayer. There was nothing urgent; they had just decided we should drop everything else because they said to.

The room began to spin, and I started to black out. I cried, "Kent, get me out of here. This is not God!"

He took me home and the light dawned on him. He made a list of all the spirits he felt were operating over the four of us, called the couple, and said if they weren't willing to rebuke all these spirits and never operate that way again, he and I were out of the covenant. They replied that since we never included the ministry, it wasn't really a covenant and left us holding all the debts.

I have nothing against this couple. We were all in deception. I relate it now only to help anyone who might read this to be alert to a similar trap that the devil might be setting. He has no new tricks, only different packages.

So many Christians like myself, get born-again and lose all logic. We want to serve God so zealously that we run off to do whatever seems like God's work without first getting rooted and grounded in the Word. We're willing to sacrifice all personal comfort and, without knowledge of God's Word, we also give up all common sense, and the devil chuckles while we spin our wheels thinking we're serving God. It's great to want to be more than a pew warmer, but I wish I had followed Jesus' and Paul's examples. They both worked and studied the Word and got in step with God's timing before they launched their ministries. They didn't do too badly either.

A couple of months after the covenant broke up, Linus, our business manager, came tearing up the stairs yelling, "Red alert. Red alert! Shirley Boone is on the phone!"

Pat Boone had been my teenage idol so I did the spiritual thing and turned into a pile of "Jello". I told Linus to get Kent to take the call, and I went into the other room to pray.

The first Christian book that I ever read was Pat's, *A New Song*. I had to throw a lot of rock star's music out and was thrilled that, not only could I keep Pat's book, but could admire his and Shirley's example as a Christian family.

I had met Pat briefly several years before at a Christian function in Omaha and had handed him one of my yellow books. I was thrilled to receive a letter from him saying he admired our cause and my book. I never had any more contact, but I still had that treasured letter. And now Shirley was on the phone. She ordered some of our tapes that day. She and Pat had experienced Jesus' healing power in their own marriage and have a real desire to see families healed. Soon she called back and said, "Let's do a marriage-healing seminar right here in Hollywood in the heart of the devil's territory where he is glorifying divorce. Will you come to our home?"

We didn't have to search our calendars. We just said, "Yes, we will be there."

They invited southern California church leaders, friends, and a few movie stars, some with broken marriages. We always ministered from two directors' chairs which had our names on the back. Shirley sat us on top of a huge coffee table in their family room which held about fifty people.

"TOTALLY AWESOME," if I may borrow a phrase from the teenagers, is the only way I can describe the experience. I would've paid money to see Pat anywhere, but here he was, perched on a stool listening to me for five nights! And right at my feet on the front row sat one of my family's most favorite T.V. stars who actually laughed at all my little jokes. I had to ask God to help me to remember what I was there for rather than get off my chair and ask for autographs. The last night, Pat and their daughter, Debby, sang. It was glorious. I wept and didn't want it to end.

Imagine how I felt: My "energy crisis" had begun to lessen. I had been transported from deathly-tired covenant member in Nowhere, Iowa, whose opinion wasn't worth hearing, to guest speaker in the Beverly Hills home of my teenage hero who payed attention to every word I said for a week! I couldn't believe it. Both Pat and Shirley counted me as an equal in every conversation. Movie stars were taking time to come listen to me! It was pretty heady stuff, but it only served to humble me before God. Only He could have been responsible for such a transformation in my life, and I knew it.

We stayed with Boones all during the seminar and they opened their home to us whenever we came to Southern California. I've watched these two people really live what they preach. It's not that they never have problems. On the contrary. However, I found they were not so image-conscious or "holier than thou", so to speak, as to be afraid to talk openly about their problems. They are very transparent. With Pat and Shirley, "What you see is what you get," and I love them very much for that. I only wish now that I had had the freedom to follow their example.

Soon after the seminar, Pat and Shirley had us as their guests on the Praise The Lord broadcast on the Trinity network which they often hosted for the founders, Paul and Jan Crouch.

Little did I dream how the ministry would grow due to our involvement with the Boones. I was only aware of feeling incredibly honored to be allowed to serve God in this way. My tears of frustration had turned to tears of joy.

Me with Pat Boone.

7

MINISTRY FLOURISHES, MARRIAGE FALTERS

The Boones recorded the seminar we did in their home and made it into an album called *"Our Marriage Covenant"*. We did several guest appearances with them on T.B.N., and the albums began selling like hotcakes. Pat and Shirley got letters, and we got letters saying how much the album helped their marriage. God really blessed that seminar.

We had so many Standers' groups forming in southern California that we flew out to Beverly Hills every six weeks to hold regular meetings. We appeared on the Praise the Lord broadcast each time.

Most of the people who attended our meetings were halves of couples praying for their partners to come home. First, we always worshipped with beautiful Holy Spirit-led musicians. Then reunited couples would tell how their marriages got healed. Each story had its own unique moments of tears and laughter, and we fell in love with each couple who shared. Kent and I usually had a teaching, and then we would pray for anyone afterward. We never knew who might show up. Once Pat and Shirley dropped in after a Hollywood function and surprised us all. Gavin and Patti Mac Leod became almost regulars before and after their remarriage. Most important of all, people were getting born-again and marriages **were** being healed. That's what kept me going because I never did learn to like packing up and leaving my kids.

Why, I do not know, but God used to do special things for me personally when I went to California. It was like He was saying, "Here's a surprise I planned for you to let you know I appreciate what you're doing for Me." I never could figure it out because He knew I'd do anything just to serve Him, but I believe He wants us to know He really is our Father, our "Daddy", not just our heavenly taskmaster. After all, Dads like to have fun with their kids. I really became aware that God loved me and didn't just need me to work for Him.

For instance, it couldn't have been just a coincidence that this star-struck kid got to spend three birthdays in a row at Pat and Shirley's. They always had a lovely gift for me and took me out to dinner. I used to wonder if Pat had any inkling when he sang "Happy Birthday" to me that he magically changed in my mind from the dear friend he had become back into my teenage heart throb. I still couldn't believe Pat Boone was singing to me in that voice that caused me to save my allowances to buy all his records from the time I was fourteen. What precious moments.

As a small child, I idolized Roy Rogers. I bought his comic books and copied pictures of Roy and Trigger. One evening as Shirley and I were putting on our mikes to do a Praise the Lord show, a note from the audience was slipped into my hand.

It was from a lady saying her marriage had been healed through the Boone seminar tapes. Incidentally, she is Dale Evans' granddaughter.

I went out to meet her after the show, and we began getting together every time we came to California. We became fast friends. When she and her husband found out how I adored Roy and Dale, they asked if I'd like to tour the Roy Rogers Museum. Does a bear like honey? Of course, I wanted to go so they drove us up to Apple Valley. When I walked in,

I got all teary just looking at all the Roy Rogers memorabilia. But when, to my amazement, Roy and Dale walked in, I went weak, and the tears just streamed! I was totally speechless as Roy hugged us and said he was taking us out to lunch. By the time Dale announced we would spend the afternoon at their house, I think I managed to close my mouth and act semi-intelligent. I glanced at my friends and they were grinning from ear to ear. They, of course, had set this all up for me. Later that day, Roy took me to the room where all his old costumes are hanging, and I could scarcely believe I was actually touching the fringed shirts, boots, and guns, that I used to draw meticulously as a child.

I soaked in every word as Roy told about when he bought Trigger and Dale told about falling in love with Roy as his leading lady. They are so warm and down-to-earth that I soon found my tongue but, at the same time, was so thrilled I was almost beside myself. Roy said not to think I was strange. Even grown-up men get all teary when they meet him because he brings their childhood back to them.

Think about the heart of God. My heavenly Father had this all planned for me when I was a little girl on a farm in Iowa drawing pictures of my favorite cowboy.

That night we were staying with a dear friend, Janeen. She and Kent went to a meeting, but I was so wound up and worn out that I stayed home alone and tuned into T.B.N. A handsome, Black Gospel singer was on. The love of Jesus so radiated from his face that I made careful note of his name, Howard McCrary, and asked God out loud to please let me hear him in person some day.

The Lord must've really chuckled at that prayer. The very next evening, we arrived at the Century Plaza Hotel to do our meeting, and a Black preacher friend met us saying something about Howard McCrary! My heart skipped a beat, and I said, "What about Howard McCrary?" He answered, "Why, didn't you know? Howard is my brother-in-law, and he's doing your music tonight!"

Once again, I just threw my hands up in awe and said, "Lord, how can You be so good to me?"

The ministry was growing so large that we couldn't possibly travel to all the Standers' groups so Kent decided to hold a national convention. Our first one was in Tulsa on the 59th floor of the City of Faith. Pat and Shirley honored us by being our guest speakers. God really anointed them that night, and it was an honor to stand beside them as the four of us prayed for all the dear people who were able to attend.

Another time we met in Christ Chapel at O.R.U., and Shirley was our guest speaker. Oral and Evelyn Roberts came and sat on the front row. I will never forget Kent's mother as Oral sat down beside her. She didn't move a muscle, but her face began to glow as though heaven had come down.

At that convention, we asked people to pray about helping us buy an office building because the basement of our home was becoming very overcrowded. Our volunteers barely had room to turn around without stumbling over one another. The phone counselors couldn't hear with the tape duplicators running so close by.

We had located a perfect-sized building on the town square which quite a few local businessmen were also interested in buying. When Oral Roberts stood up and gave us $11,000, which was the down payment we needed to the penny, I think I held on to Shirley to keep from falling off the stage.

I never could quite believe that all this was happening to me, a little girl from the Iowa corn fields. This had to be God, didn't it?

There were still parts of my marriage that weren't healed, but I had shoved them to the background because I told myself they were immaterial compared to the spectacular things that were happening in the ministry. Not only that, but we were so busy dealing with other people's marriage problems that we didn't have time to think about our own. I think we both unconsciously played a sort of mind game: "If you don't talk about problems, then they don't exist." All that was happening in the ministry seemed so miraculous. I thought it must be God's supernatural plan for us, and my faith carried me through the problem areas. The more it appeared that God was promoting the ministry and the more marriages were healed the more I would tell myself, "I am going to get the rest of my prayer because God would not put me in a marriage-healing ministry if everything in my own marriage isn't right."

When I would read other people's marriage books, I was forced to admit, "My goodness! Ours is not complete." Then I would ask, "Kent, please read this book so we can discuss it."

Kent was a visionary. He just wanted to charge ahead and do great things for God. He'd say, "Oh, you read it for me and tell me about it."

He was very content to teach the things that we had learned and just stop there. As long as the ministry seemed so successful, and people never seemed to tire of hearing the things we taught, what else did we need? He also didn't have time to do everything there was to do with the ministry growing like it was. I don't think I even let myself realize how our home life was being put on the back burner for the ministry.

We moved into our new headquarters. We had been operating debt-free and had saved up $2,500 for furniture. We had been running on a shoe-string so that seemed like a fortune. We went to a used-furniture auction to buy a few desks and chairs to put in this building, which granted, was going to be quite empty for a while but I didn't care. It was such luxury compared to our basement. Our business manager, Linus, and his wife, Kay, went with us to the auction. We got some really good deals, but the $2,500 was gone in no time. There were so many other good bargains to be auctioned off, and we had many rooms to fill so Kent disappeared and made a call to a banker in Council Bluffs. The banker was fascinated to see how our ministry had grown, and over the phone he okayed a loan for $6,000 to buy more furniture. Kent came back and said, "Go on. Make bids for whatever you want. I've got $6,000."

I sank on the inside. I thought, "Oh no, we're off into borrowing in the ministry again. We're buying something that we don't have money for. Where is it going to come from?"

Kent thought that since God gave us the building, God

would give us the money to fill it with furniture. I did too, but I thought we should have waited till the cash came and not borrow, but it was too late. We launched off the new building this way, and the pattern never ended.

I began to just bury myself in studying the Bible. I was trying to figure out what seemed to me to be an enigma in the Scriptures. Jesus seemed to say unconditionally, if people remarry, they are in adultery, but what did that really mean? Anyone could see that God was blessing second, third, and fourth marriages. I was trying to blend what I could observe from real life with what the Scriptures said because I was the writer of the ministry.

Research, traveling, preaching and taking care of my girls was my life. Kristin was a teenager, and helped me so much with little Mandy. They were very important to me. I don't think I would have survived without a nervous break-down without Kristin's help. From time to time I would notice that the ministry was taking all of Kent's time. I had prayed him out of adultery with other women in order to share him with thousands of other women all over the country who were Standers, who lived for him to come and build up their faith. He was their model of the ideal husband they were all praying for. I rebuked the devil whenever resentment came and scolded myself that I couldn't complain about the ministry's needs intruding into our personal life.

The development of the ministry was Kent's. He would stay up all hours dreaming up new "arms" of ministry. He saw needs everywhere and thought our ministry should meet them. He formed an arm of ministry called "Prepared Partners" for engaged couples. Another arm was called "Repairers and Restorers". It consisted of fasting brigades all over the United States that fasted for one another's marriage to be healed. The most famous arm of ministry was "The Standers." There was also "Nova Shalom," the Greek word "nova" meaning new and "shalom", the Hebrew word for peace...New Peace. That was for married couples who were both interested in strengthening their marriages. Kent collaborated with the couple who headed this arm to write a thirteen-week curriculum on spiritual principles in marriage that were studied in a leader's home. The couples were also given homework. They were supposed to live the principle they studied all week long. That arm of ministry split off from "Born Again Marriages" with our blessing, several years ago. Nova Shalom is successful to this day and has witnessed the healing of a lot of marriages.

Kent also got a "message from God" that he was going to start a church. It was going to be debt-free, struggle-free, and so successful that every denomination would be coming to him to find out how he had done it. It was going to be the example for the "last days" churches. He had no trouble imagining this, but I sure did. I didn't get any witness to it whatsoever. Kent finally decided to wait until I got a witness on it because I reacted so strongly which was unusual for me.

We were still being controlled by these messages that I am now convinced came from a familiar spirit, for the most part. When they first starting coming, they were scriptural and actually helped us work out problems in our marriage. They planted the idea that, at the drop of a hat, we could call on God by praying in tongues and God would give us a special message. We taught couples everywhere we went to sit down and pray in the Spirit and wait for God to speak. God only knows how many people have been similarly misguided because of our teaching. I don't mean to say God never talks to you when you pray but it usually won't be pages every time you pray.

So many of the messages would be absolutely earth-shaking, of world and national importance. Part of the reason I felt I could never ask for a rest or object to anything was because according to these messages, the United States would fall if the marriages don't get healed, and our ministry was the last-day ministry called to put the marriages of this country together. This was such a tremendous responsibility, I felt I had to sacrifice everything personal so we would not fail God and this country.

With a belief like that, there isn't a personal problem that is important. I can hardly believe that I lived that way. I literally did not have any right to complain or put up any strong objections to anything.

81

At least our ministry never wrote any 'faith checks'. People in the world have enough sense to know when you write a check without enough money in the bank to cover it, that is not a "faith check", that is a "hot check". No wonder non-Christians laugh at us. We Christians tend to lose all logic and think it is faith. Whenever our "faith" seems to go against all principles of integrity, it is not faith, it is foolishness! I helped Kent write a book called *To Boredom And Back*. The book was about the healing of our marriage from his standpoint. It included all of the Scriptural principles we used that other people could use to get their marriages healed. We had a ready market for it since we sold it at our meetings and told about it on television. People not only bought it for themselves but bought dozens of copies for their friends and relatives.

I could never convince our ministry to get a financial advisor so I learned to live without opening any mail that looked like bills or ever asking to see the ministry's books. I had decided that I would just wash my hands of the finances. I came to the point of not even wanting to hear about it because I couldn't sleep at night if I did. I would get up on the stage and wonder, "Who is going to get hurt financially by being involved in this ministry?" and then condemn myself for such a rotten attitude!

Couples were moving in from out of state to get involved with the ministry, and I would think, "Dear God, are they going to get hurt? They've sold their home to come here. What is going to happen to them if we can't pay their salary?"

This never worried Kent in the least. He always felt God would take care of them. I was never sure God wanted them to come so I couldn't quit worrying.

At our conventions, I stood on the stage smiling radiantly thinking, "All these hundreds of people would not be here if they knew how financially unsound we are."

I felt I could tell no one or they'd think I was just being "sour grapes" or that I was not behind the ministry. I got very good at flashing smiles on stage and on camera whether I felt like it or not. Sometimes we had big long offerings where people would give not only money but their jewelry. I felt so phony standing on the stage in my pretty dress with my daughters in their pretty dresses with my plastic smile on my face, while inside I was dying of fear that some people were going to be hurt financially or were giving out of emotion when they shouldn't be. I would pray that the Boones would not be hurt in their financial involvement with us in producing the *"Marriage Covenant"* tape and albums at their home. All the while, I forced the plastic smile and kept quiet because I thought there was something wrong with MY attitude toward the ministry, and I begged God to fix ME!

No matter how much money came in, the ministry always seemed to have need for more. Kent always sincerely believed that God would keep providing and eventually provide more than enough so that we could pay off the debts and go on. We never spent money frivolously or "lined our own pockets". We had a set personal salary which we did't get unless employees were all paid first.

Constantly aware of the snowballing ministry debt, several times I objected strongly to always being behind, Kent would say, "Your duty is to pray, support, praise, and adore me. That is your whole job in life. Leave business things up to me."

And so I did. I should have taken the authority I had as Vice President of the ministry and refused to operate that way any longer. At that time I couldn't begin to contemplate such bold action.

If I raised a question about anything, I was criticizing, complaining, and nagging. This was not what we taught on stage. We portrayed that we agreed on everything, but that was in the past. Now I felt completely stifled.

I know now that submission should not be blind, ignorant, or unwarranted submission. Submission is not an end but a means to an end. The end is peace, harmony, happiness, security, and other things of ultimate value to the marriage and family. I don't believe a husband should have to demand submission from his wife. I believe it is warranted by his wise leadership and loving care for his family.

Wives, it is equally wrong for you to be aggressive or

overbearing in expressing your opinions. That causes husbands to feel they have to assert themselves as your head or flaunt the "submission clause". Both are extremes! Both are a misuse of Scripture and destructive to a marriage relationship. I am not now anti-submission. I am anti-destruction. The ministry was growing at such a rate that now we no hardly had time to sit down and pray. Kent said he didn't have time to call me about every decision. The wheels of the ministry were grinding along. I had the sensation they were grinding me to a pulp and I was powerless to stop them.

Kent was afraid to have a board of directors because he had heard that boards have taken over the leadership of the ministry. So our board consisted of Kent and me, nobody else, and I had no voice in running it. We never did have counselors of any sort. We had quarterly leaders' meetings where I got run through the wringer with all our leaders' complaints. I finally didn't even want to go to those meetings because they were such a power struggle.

The ministry was becoming, for me, like a big steam roller.
It very obviously no longer mattered what I said or how I felt. I was just a figure head.

It was beginning to dawn on me that we now had a ministry but no longer a marriage. I was a married single and Kent was married to the ministry. But... we now had thousands of people who were depending on us because of television exposure. I couldn't express any displeasure. I felt I had to live for these people because that was the call God had on my life. We were "the perfect couple" that everyone wished they could be. I didn't want to wreck their faith or disappoint anyone, especially God. They loved us, and I loved them, but I wondered how long I could keep on living a lie to please people.

8

THE CAPTAIN
AND HIS MATE

Gavin MacLeod, who played the captain on the long-running T.V. series, THE LOVE BOAT, had divorced his wife Patti three years prior to our coming to Beverly Hills. Patti was broken-hearted and had recently become a Christian. Someone had given her my "Yellow Book" in New York, and when she returned to L.A., she called Shirley Boone and asked, "Shirley, how can I meet these Axtells?"

"Patti, you won't believe this, but Kent and Dru Axtell are guests in our home this very moment. They are doing a meeting tonight, and you need to go to it. I will arrange a personal counseling session with Dru," Shirley replied.

Patti MacLeod is a sweet lady who had survived those three years by being in a group called L.A.D.I.E.S., which stood for "Life After Divorce Is Eventually Sane."

At the time when Gavin divorced Patti, it seemed like there was an epidemic of Hollywood divorces. The ex-wives of these famous men, to help keep their sanity, banded together and formed this group. They got national acclaim, appeared on talk shows, and so on. They had all decided to go on with their lives, except Patti, who could not seem to cope without Gavin. She had tried dating, but she couldn't stand it. She loved Gavin. She had accepted Christ after their divorce and had read the "Yellow Book". She came to our meeting that night in Beverly Hills. Afterwards we met and spoke privately. She was so sad and worn out. She said that she had cried almost every day for three years.

As I looked into her face and saw the lines pain had etched and eyes that would overflow with tears as she spoke, I desperately hoped God was, indeed, behind our getting together. I had seen enough by now to know all marriages did not get healed, but I did not have the freedom to say so publicly.

I taught her how to pray in faith, and we prayed together for the healing of hers and Gavin's marriage. She then began to thank God every day for Gavin coming home. I implored God not to let me lead her down a rosy path to nowhere as I felt she couldn't take much more.

About four weeks later, after three years of not one word of communication, Gavin called Patti. He said that he thought that they should be friends and asked if he could come to see her. Imagine Patti's excitement. She said, "Of course, Gavin. I would love to see you. Why don't you come for dinner?"

When Gavin arrived at her door, in a moment of humor Patti said, "Welcome home, Gavin. Your dinner is cold. It's been waiting three years!"

They talked, laughed, cried, hugged, and talked some more. Several hours passed. Gavin had come over just to be friends. However, by the time he left, he knew that they belonged together.

Kent and I returned to Beverly Hills a couple of weeks later. Gavin and Patti both came to our meeting. Afterward, we went to his beautiful home up in the canyon. I will never forget it. It was just like a dream. I couldn't believe that God would use us to help bring healing to this famous couple. Gavin showed us around his absolutely gorgeous home. We went out to the sunken pool. The moonlight was shimmering on the water when Gavin put his arms around Patti and kissed her. It was so romantic, and I said, "Gavin, this is just like a scene on THE LOVE BOAT!"

He looked down at Patti and said with feeling, "Yes, but this is real."

These were beautiful times. We talked about the Bible until the wee hours. Gavin was so eager to learn and so very hungry for God.

We advised them, "Don't get remarried right away. Let's root out the problems that hurt your marriage in the first place so when you remarry, you can make it."

We gave them better advice than we experienced ourselves. Every six weeks when we visited them in Beverly Hills, God would have new instructions for Gavin. Bless his heart, he carried each one out and they weren't always easy. He would say, "What can I do? Show me what to do, and I will do it."

The day after Gavin got baptized in the Spirit, he was praying in tongues on the way to the studio where they taped THE LOVE BOAT. God spoke to him, "Don't worry about when to get remarried. I will tell you."

So the pressure was gone. They came to every one of our Beverly Hills meetings. Usually people would beg them to come on stage and tell a word of encouragement which they gladly did. After each meeting, we would go out for dinner and fellowship. What good times we had. Sometimes Gavin and Patti would lapse into one of their old theatre routines and we'd watch, enchanted. I got used to fans flocking around Gavin for autographs and was delighted to find out he is a humble man. Once he told me he always wondered why they gave the part of the captain to him when there were other guys who had lots of hair. Now he knew God had done it to give him a platform to witness for Jesus - and witness he does! I grew to love him and Patti dearly.

Nine months later we were getting ready to have our third annual Born-Again Marriages Convention when Gavin said, "Why don't Patti and I fly up to Omaha so you can remarry us at your convention? Wouldn't that build faith in all of your followers?"

We said, "It certainly would."

(Left to right) Me, Kent, Gavin, Patti, Dean
and Sandy Brown, Shirley and Pat Boone.

Patti and Mandy before the big wedding.
Mandy was flower girl.

They said, "Don't go to any trouble. We will just sit in the audience. You can call us up front and marry us." (Kent and I were both ordained ministers.)

I flew home with one week to prepare for a movie star's wedding! We already had the auditorium rented. I added some beautiful lacy lawn furniture, an arch with ferns, baby's breath, and flowers all over the place. It looked like a fairyland. Patti and Gavin were so surprised. They didn't expect us to make a big deal out of it whatsoever. My best friend, Rita, was on hand to do Patti's hair and make-up. Mandy was the flower girl and adorable, if I do say so myself. Pat and Shirley Boone flew in to stand up with them and sang romantic songs, wedding songs, and Gospel songs. Sandy Brown, a lady evangelist friend of ours, who was influential in Gavin's early Christian walk, did the preaching. Kent and I performed the marriage ceremony. Pat served communion to the whole audience of about a thousand people who thought they were just coming to the regular opening night of our convention. They had no idea that they were coming to a movie star's wedding! Gavin did not want any Hollywood flash bulb effect so we couldn't tell anybody about the wedding. It still made headlines in all of the national newspapers and magazines. It was one of the most thrilling events in which I was ever privileged to participate. The presence of the Lord seemed to permeate the entire wedding. It was beautiful from start to finish.

Patti and Gavin said their own vows to each other, and they after the actual ceremony was over, both gave their testimonies. Then all of us on stage pitched in with humorous and touching anecdotes. It was a four-and-a-half hour wedding, and no one wanted it to end. As Pat and Shirley were singing some old love songs, Patti whispered to me, "Dru, this is just like a Betty Grable movie."

Patti and Gavin's reunion has been one of the most rewarding healed marriages that resulted from our ministry. They have gone on to serve the Lord whole-heartedly. Both of them are very bold witnesses for Jesus wherever they go.

After that, the ministry took off like a rocket. With all the publicity in major newspapers, magazines, and Hollywood tabloids, it seemed as though everybody wanted our books and tapes. We hated to turn down orders if enough money didn't come in, so the charging and borrowing continued to escalate.

Meanwhile, I was feeling more and more like a married single. The kids and I were like stage props. We would get all dressed up and sit on a stage looking pretty, typifying the model Christian family. "But we have no family life," was secret thought.

I would ask myself over and over, "This has to be God... doesn't it?"

After all, we couldn't make all this happen ourselves. Who was I to fight God? I was so unhappy. I cried out, "God, I have movie stars for friends. Some of the finest homes in Hollywood are open to me. I have beautiful Christian friends, and my family is together so, Jesus, what else are You going to have to do for me to make me truly happy? I am glad for the good things that are happening with You, Lord, but it seems like my own marriage is just a tool for the ministry. What is wrong with me to be so selfish and ungrateful?"

I always blamed me. I never thought that it was someone else's fault. I would ask, "What is wrong with me, Lord?" and I never seemed to get an answer.

Finally, one day I did realize that all I ever really wanted was a husband who wanted to come home to me. That's what I had prayed for, and that's why I wasn't happy even with all the blessings that come from helping couples reunite.

At this time, Kent was asked to write an article for *Ministries Magazine*. He wrote that God is first, marriage is second, and the ministry is third. I remember proofing and editing it for him and saying, "Why are you writing this? We aren't living it. I don't know any minister who is living it. Why is everyone going around preaching that this is the order when no one is living it? This article is a sham." I was becoming more and more puzzled about the whole thing.

After Gavin and Patti's wedding, Jan and Paul Crouch decided that we should have our own T.V. show. Jan and Paul have a real heart for marriage healing. They asked, "Would you be willing to come out here and do a show that you would host and direct? We would like you to interview couples you know with healed marriages. We will pay the bill.''

I said I would as long as I didn't have to ask for money and if the show was going to be more than light-hearted entertainment. I wanted to do nitty-gritty stuff that would really help people. I wanted people to be able to tune in the show and hear something they could put into action that very day to help their marriage.

Jan and Paul said that was what they wanted too.

We did the first show on the bow of a yacht with our friends, Todd and Candie Halberg. I had been on television shows quite a bit, but this was different. The camera was on one yacht we were on another. It would go up when we would go down. I knew that if I tipped my chair at all, I would end up in the harbor. But Todd and Candi have a great testimony, and soon I got into their story and relaxed.

I had been so nervous. Paul and Jan were investing a lot of money to do our show. I desperately did not want to disappoint them or God.

Kent wanted to call the show "Even in Hollywood", but Jan Crouch said that the Lord told her to call it, "Marriage on the Rock" (the Rock meaning Jesus). I loved the title and knew that Jan had heard from God so that was the name of our show. We flew to California every six weeks and taped twelve or thirteen shows at a time. It was my job to put together twelve coordinated outfits for each of us every trip. I had to shop at discount houses but I enjoyed every minute of it.

I never regretted doing a single one of those shows. Each one had its own unique message and personality. Every couple was lovely to work with. I don't believe that we taught any wrong doctrines. They were real life experiences that said, "This is what God did for this couple, and it's possible that He could do the same for you."

We did some shows in Pat and Shirley's back yard and also in Gavin and Patti's Santa Monica apartment. We taped all over, but finally we settled down to a quaint hotel called the Seal Beach Inn. The owner, Mrs. Bettenhausen, which incidentally means "house of beds", a sweet Christian lady, was doing her dishes one day when the Lord spoke to her and said, "I want you to establish a Christian Inn."

She uniquely furnished every room with hand-picked European antiques. It was the most charming place, with its many nooks, crannies, and beds of sweet-scented flowers blooming everywhere. The guests were thrilled to stay there while we were shooting. They all declared it was like a second honeymoon.

Jan and Paul sent out a mobile TV unit that was state of the art equipment. One thing about the Crouches; they do things right! The crew that we worked with were wonderful, and they knew what they were doing. I soon learned that you had to make up more heavily for those bright lights. Sometimes ladies who had never been on TV would come on the show without a stitch of makeup on. I learned to invite them very tactfully to allow me to do their make-up so that the camera lights would not wash them out. Even that part was fun for me.

Mrs. Bettenhausen had bicycles at the inn, and while the crew would set up to shoot, I would go riding by the ocean and pray, to prepare for the show. I loved doing it. I really believe there was a real anointing on the show.

When we would interview a couple and they would sit there with love in their eyes, holding hands, I would often be unable to stop the tears from running down my face. People would think that I was crying because of the beautiful poignant story that was being told. I hoped no one knew that, in reality, I was crying because of the glaring difference in their marriage and ours. Here we were hosting this show, and I was feeling more and more like a phony.

The couples would enjoy the romance of the inn and make intimate remarks to one another about what a great time they had sleeping on silk sheets with the scent of honeysuckle wafting through the air. I went there to work; I did not go there to be romantic because we did not have any romance. I was feeling the lack of it, but I didn't know what to do. Kent was feeling the lack of it too because he would tell me I was not a good lover. I was frustrated with myself because the feelings were not there and I knew that I was not a good lover but issuing commands and put-downs was not exactly the way to get love out of me. I didn't know what to do about it. If it didn't come naturally, I couldn't seem to phony it up so I was never good enough. I knew the Scriptures said that if a wife holds back sex, she is defrauding her partner so I would initiate it and do my best to be a good sex partner. I wanted it to work. I had based my belief on the teaching that if I did what I was supposed to do, the feelings would follow but I was getting more disillusioned by the day.

I would like to quote from the *Hidden Christian* by Cliff Dudley, New Leaf Press, Inc.

"Today many marriages are based on eros love alone. The partners soon discover that after the "act" there are still 23½ hours left in each day that they must live in harmony with their mates. Zap! They can't. The result is a 52% divorce rate for "Christian" marriages.

"However, on the other end of the scale, many today are marrying because, 'our spirits bear witness that we are the sons of God,' only to discover that there is no phileo or eros love, and they, too, end up in a life of misery or one of the 52% divorce statistics.

"As the writer of the article stated, 'We are commanded by Christ to see one another as valuable and precious.' It is fine and good for us to realize that, but that certainly isn't love. Love is action and emotion added to agape.

"Love without action and emotions is as dead as faith without works.

"I would like to see a love relationship where the senses are deadened. What wife would be pleased if the husband didn't ever love her with his senses - never look at her, never talk to her, never notice how wonderful she smells. That can never be! It is time we stand against the devil and move in faith in our love relationships.

"If we were only spirits, the agape love alone would be enough to fulfill us as mankind."

What I did was zero in on the fact that marriages had to have the agape (God-kind of love) and the phileo (friendship). Since there was no eros, I thought that we could make it without it.

Most Christians have had teaching on the fact that we are a three-part being: body, soul and spirit. We cannot separate them; they are all inter-twined. To try to ignore the physical aspect of marriage and just live on the spiritual and soul part is impossible if a marriage is to be a fulfilling one. I thought maybe the excitement and the rewards of the ministry would make up for some of the areas that were lacking in our marriage because, God knows, I did love seeing other people get their marriages healed.

I believe we need all three kinds of love to start a marriage relationship: eros, phileo, and agape. True, in the world, most people are doing without agape, but I went off the deep end the other way and figured that we could do without eros. Certainly feelings are not our ultimate guide but God created us with feelings. We would be very hard, cold individuals without them. The trick, I believe, is not to deny their existence but to compare what we are feeling with Scripture and not allow our feelings to cause us to blatantly sin. Everything looked so good on the outside. We were doing meetings in the grandest hotels. We would go downtown to the Beverly Hills Theater, and there on the marquee would be: BORN-AGAIN MARRIAGES WITH GAVIN AND PATTI MACLEOD. Gavin and Patti thought that it was just wonderful that we were having a born-again function in that old theater.

In those meetings, our habit was to ask all of the couples whose marriages were healed to stand up. There could be five hundred people there, and if we were fortunate, five to eight healed marriages would stand up. Everybody would go wild and cheer and clap for them. Maybe we would have one or two of them come up on stage and give their testimony, which was always a fun thing.

For some reason my eyes would be drawn to that sea of faces that didn't stand up, didn't raise their hands, and hadn't had their marriage healed. I would see the pain, the hurt, and the fear in their eyes. I would stand up there saying on the inside, "God, am I giving these people false hopes? Am I teaching off doctrine? Are all of these people really going to get their marriages healed?"

By then we had been in the ministry for eleven or twelve years, and I had time to watch real life being lived. I knew of Godly men and women who'd been standing six, eight, ten years whose partners had remarried and had children. I secretly felt they were wasting their lives to wait any longer, but did God feel that way, too? Would I be wrecking their faith to tell them to quit standing? Gavin and Patti's reuniting had caused a bitter-sweet reaction for many of those praying for their marriages to be healed. Sweet, because they were so thrilled for Patti and Gavin. Bitter, because some had prayed for years so why did Patti get her prayers answered in only a month? Didn't God love them as much? Was their faith too weak? These were some of the questions I was asked by people with pain in their eyes. I had no answers for them. Their faces haunted me. I had no idea how to bridge the gap between faith and foolishness. I was sure many were living in a fantasy world that we had created for them. How could I tell them without tearing those off their "stand" that was of God? I began frantically crying out to God to tell me what was wrong and how to fix it.

9

I THOUGHT
IT WAS GOD

I knew the loneliness that could overcome a person trying to adjust to living alone after being married. I personally didn't know how some of the sweet people involved in our ministry could stand in faith for one, two, five, eight, even ten years...alone...waiting for their partner to come home.

It began to trouble me that I could be responsible for them not going on with their lives. Some of them, I was sure, were in a fantasy, not faith "standing" while their partners were, in most cases, happily remarried for years-perhaps with several children. There had to be an answer between law and grace. We taught everyone to stand for the healing of their marriage. And we taught that remarriage was adultery! Yet, in real life, I could see God blessing remarriages and forgiving divorce. The first four verses of Deuteronomy 24, which allowed divorce, plagued me. Would Jesus place harsher laws on His new covenant people than Moses gave to those under the old covenant? Surely not, and Jesus said He did not come to do away with the Law and Moses.

I had to face facts. Some people's marriages were not being healed. Everybody in our ministry explained it away by rationalizing that they didn't "stand" long enough or they got lonely and gave up or their faith level was not strong enough.

Many times there was great condemnation from ministry members on someone who claimed that God said they were free and didn't have to stand any more. I knew I didn't have all the answers, but somehow condemning those who chose to stop waiting for their ex-spouse didn't seem like a Holy Spirit leading.

So many Christians involved in our ministry would rather suffer than admit that they were perhaps walking in error. I knew that unless they got some Holy Spirit revelation on what Jesus really meant concerning divorce and remarriage that many would stay in the bondage of HAVING to stand even if their spouse had been remarried for many years. On the surface it seems so cut and dried...remarriage is adultery. But Jesus clearly did not come to make a fool out of Moses who allowed divorce without repercussions. And think of this: The God who can forgive murder (Moses) and adultery (David), can also forgive a marriage failure.

The capstone for me was realizing that God planned Jesus' genealogy before the foundation of the world and He allowed Jesus to be a direct descendant of Solomon who was born to David with the ex-wife of Uriah.

Don't say, "That relationship was also adultery so does that also justify adultery?" Of course not! God was showing the totality of His forgiveness to David after he repented.

I have been on a research mission for the whole fourteen years of my Christian walk reading every book I could find on the subject of Christ's sayings about divorce and remarriage, not to mention going over and over the Scriptures and praying for revelation. I doubt if any of us will have absolute understanding of the mind of Christ on this subject until we can sit at His feet and learn. However, I would like to share quotes from several authors that I believe contain some of the most viable interpretations I have found to date.

At this point, let me warn you I switch from my autobiographical style to some "heavy" theology. You will not get

98

the full import of these passages by skimming over them. Please reset your computer, shift gears, and prepare to slow down and STUDY. You may want to come back to them again and again.

First, let me quote from my son-in-law, Peter Norville's thesis, written while attending Oral Roberts University, entitled *The Heart of Divorce*, concerning Jesus' statements on divorce and remarriage in Matthew 5:31-32:

> Jesus was seeking the creation of one-flesh couples who understood His demand for new marriage relationships because of removing the "hard heart" and not because of attaining the Law. Jesus was saying that legalism must be done away with while, at the same time, a standard must remain. An indication that a battle still rages between the legalism of the Law and the gift of the Gospel is the persecution existing towards those who have been divorced. Jesus said in Matthew 5:22 and 28 that anger and lust are sins just as he says divorce is sin; but He was not making a distinction between sins like many do. The fact that the divorce occasion is more easily prosecuted than perhaps lust or anger, opens the door to a legalistic approach. If one misinterprets this point, one will also likely misinterpret the "except clause" legalistically, thus making a provision for divorce. This use of the "except clause" would be born out of one's own stringent approach and would contradict the divine ideal to which Jesus is pointing.

> A legalistic rendering is not what Jesus wanted to say. An illustration will help further this understanding of the difference between the Gospel intent and the legalistic Law. The legalistic Law could be equated with a wall and fulfilling the Law's requirements equated with reaching the top of the wall. Scripture states that all fall short of attaining these requirements (Romans 3:23). Indeed, anyone who has read the Gospels, or specifically the Sermon on the Mount, as Law will soon recog-

nize the impossibility of reaching the top of the wall by keeping all of its requirements. Yet, Jesus still demands that one's righteousness surpass that of the Pharisees (Matthew 5:20) and that not one command be broken (Matthew 5:19). Between the conflict of the Law and the Gospel, an answer emerges.

Jesus, bringing the Gospel of the Kingdom of God, still wants His disciples to live up to the high standards that He is instituting. Therefore, He positions Himself on top of the wall of legalistic requirements in order to indicate to His followers what their goal should be. As one begins to move toward the standard, one will notice Christ's hand extended to assist. This is the Gospel's prevision in opposition to a self-righteous attainment of legalistic ordinances. One must realize his inability to live up to Christ's demands in his own strength and, in so doing, come to grips with a Gospel that calls one blessed for accepting his conditions as "poor in spirit" (Matthew 5:3). Man's inability to live up to the requirements of Christ does not keep him from entering the Kingdom of God, but his refusal to accept Christ's extended hand may. Christ has met all men where they are by extending His hand and, in so doing, He has offered a relationship within which they can work together to reach the top of the wall.

This is a demonstration of the Kingdom of God being "already" but "not yet". Christ is demanding that His disciples live free from divorce but not insisting that it be an "entrance requirement" to the Kingdom. Christ knew that even though His disciples had a "new heart" (Ezekial 36:26) they would not be free from the element of sin. Aware of this, Christ does not excuse it but rather offers hope and help to those struggling in marriages.

Although Jesus asks His disciples to be perfect as their heavenly Father is perfect (Matthew 5:48),

He understands they have not yet been made perfect (Philippians 3:12). The possibility of one's not actualizing all of the Gospel's potential in a marriage is a reality in Christ's mind. If it was not, then Christ's Gospel would become one-sided and unforgiving in the face of failure. He would withdraw His helping hand and once again the wall would become an insurmountable legal statement, only now accompanied by a judgement. This picture of Christ is inaccurate. The authentic Gospel of Christ carries forgiveness but demands integrity with regard to sin. This integrity is not an issue that can be identified by the Law; it is, rather, a matter of the Gospel and of the heart.

This raises the question of whether Jesus meant what He said about divorce causing an adulterous situation for the woman and remarriage being adultery. Within the context of the Gospel, a definition of adultery is pivotal. Jesus' declaration that these occasions are adultery must be understood as the "intent of God" that divorce and remarriage not take place rather than as "Practical law". If His statement is taken as law, a divorced person may never remarry (perhaps even their original spouse) without adultery occurring. More insight for the definition is found in Matthew 5:28, which states that a lustful look is the equivalent of adultery. The difference between these two definitions is of the heart. A reference to Mark 7:21 portrays adultery, as well as evil thoughts, as coming from men's hearts. Apparently both the thoughts and the act of adultery stem from a problem of the heart. One should not gouge out his right eye because its existence "causes" him to look lustfully upon a woman, commit adultery, and fall short of God's intent. In the same way, one should not legalistically "gouge out" the possibility of remarriage if the occasion for their marriage "causes" one to divorce, create an adulterous situation, and fall short of God's intent. In other words, if Jesus did not actually mean to gouge out one's eyes when one looks lustfully and commits adultery in one's heart, why do legalists "gouge out" the possibility of remarriage when one falls short in a marriage due to a hard heart?

The source of the adultery is the same: the hardened heart that misses God's intent. In Jesus' eyes, to remarry is adultery because there has been a hard heart somewhere in the destruction process that has missed God's intent of permanent marriages. The error, or sin, has inevitably been in the heart. When this fact is kept in view, forgiveness for one's missing the mark of God's ideal in marriage is applied just as easily as it is when one lusts in one's heart. On the other hand, a law-centered view often tags the divorcee or the one who remarries and an "adulterer-by-willful-act" and forgiveness gets caught in the accuser's throat.

In an effort to explain why Jesus says that remarriage is adultery, some have argued that the marriage bond is indissoluble. It may, perhaps, be considered adultery in the sense that indissolubility is what God desires and expects. Likewise, Christ, in His statements about divorce and remarriage, is trying to dislodge the probability of continued divorce and remarriage because it does not stand up to the divine ideal. The indissoluble position, however, when forbidding a dissolution or remarriage places too great a weight on the legality of the marriage bond and seems to forget the context of a dynamic Gospel. Overemphasizing the legality of a marriage bond jeopardizes one's understanding of the Gospel as Gospel. The context of the Gospel is the context of the heart. Jesus saw that the Pharisees did not understand this and said to them, "You are the ones who justify yourselves in the eyes of men, but God knows your hearts..." (Luke 16:15a)

The emphasis should not be that anyone who

divorces can never remarry because God cannot allow it, but rather that divorce is not an option, possibility, concession, nor an escape. Divorce is the evidence of a failure that has taken place in the heart of sinful man. The Law still stands, however, regarding divorce. God has spoken against it. Therefore, falling short of His standard requires confessions of sin, another matter that is resolved in the heart.

Richard J. Foster says in his book, *Money, Sex, & Power*: "What we must not do is to turn these perceptive words of Jesus about remarriage into another set of soul-killing laws. We would not even consider doing that with Jesus' other sayings. If we took as law His words about eyes and hands that offend us, we would all have truncated bodies (Matt. 5:29-30). None of us would even think of turning into a new legalism Jesus' instruction not to invite friends or relatives or neighbors when we give a banquet (Luke 14:12). And we should not do that with His teaching on remarriage either. It is true that in the absolute will of God His creative intent is for marriage to be a permanent "one flesh" reality that should never be severed. But in the absolute love of God, His redemptive intent covers the brokenness of our lies and sets us free.

"We must not turn Paul's counsel to the believers at Corinth into a new legalism either. For example, some will teach that there are two and two allowable grounds for divorce: adultery, because of Jesus' statement in Matthew 5:32, and desertion, because of Paul's statement in I corinthians 7:15. Then if a woman comes in telling of marital rape and every other conceivable inhumanity, she is simply and grandly told that unless there is adultery or desertion she has no "biblical" basis for divorce. Such is the mentality (and the fatal weakness) of all attempts to turn the words of Jesus and Paul into a new legalisms.

"But if we are not given a set of rules, what guidance are we given on the question of divorce today? The first thing we can say is that God's intention from the beginning is for marriage to be a permanent "one flesh" reality. God created us male and female and we are made to go together. WE are complementaries - lifelong, permanent complementaries - and anything short of that violates God's intent.

"So, although Christians may disagree on the allowable grounds for divorce, we can all agree that divorce is akin to cutting into a living organism. We are not talking about dissolving a convenient partnership that has gone sour; it is more like amputating an arm or losing a lung. Divorce cuts into the heart and soul of a "one flesh" unity. It is possible to survive the operation, but let us be unmistakably clear that we are talking about radical surgery, not just minor outpatient care."

I think my friend, Pastor Barnett of Boise, ID, summed up the subject quite well.

"Consider carefully that in Matthew 5:19 Jesus said that everyone who looks on a woman in order to lust after her commits adultery with her in his heart. This statement cannot be understood rationally to mean that a thought not carried out as an act is necessarily as consequential as the thought and act combined, but on the surface it might look this way. **The comment simply implies a principle of uprightness without changing the law,** in order that the spirit as well as the letter of the law might be recognized. (Throughout His teachings, Jesus made many comments like these, among other things, it was His way of dealing with hypocrisy in matters of moral law.)

"Considering Matthew 19:9 in view of our comments on Jesus' declaration in Matthew 5;19, one can see that Jesus was not trying to create a new technical application for the term "adultery" but was pointing out that the lawfulness of divorce does not in and of itself make it justifiable in God's sight, for one can meet every demand of a civil law regarding divorce while trampling God's instructions about love. There, we read Matthew 19:9 as generalization, a support for the marriage contract, a rebuke of popular divorce practices, a challenge for people to examine their motivations in divorce situations, and a timely statement that the decrees of men do not provide justification when God sees evil hidden in the heart."

It is my prayer that any of you who have been in bondage to doctrines instead of hearing the heart of God for your situation will pray about the validity of the views I have shared.

Remember, I've watched God heal every kind of marriage over the last fourteen years. I'm not against standing for your marriage in any way. I'm against continuing blindly for years out of loyalty to a doctrine that may not be God's will for you at all.

God's will is for each person to pray about his individual situation until he knows God has revealed exactly what he should do. How can I say that? Because after all Paul's marriage guidelines in I Corinthians 7, the bottom line for each person is stated in verse 17: "But be sure in deciding these matters that you are living as God intended, marrying or not marrying in accordance with God's direction and help, and accepting whatever situation God has put you into. This is my rule for all the churches." (LB)

A dear friend of mine, who did not come to me but took the advice of one of our counselors, stayed with her abusive husband until she was beaten so severely she had to have surgery. When I found out from her pastor, I had to apologize to her. I never instructed any one to tell a wife that she had to stay and be beaten. Incidents like this began coming to my knowledge.

Another time I listened to leaders in our ministry debate

whether a wife of an active homosexual should submit to sex with him whenever he chose to come home to her. (This wife was a Stander.) No matter how vehemently I protested against it, saying this was now with the AIDS problem a matter of life and death, their decision was that she should submit and trust God to protect her. If we cannot see that this is foolish bondage to a doctrine then heaven help us.

I was trying to cope and cried out to God heartsick, "Please tell me if my ministry is teaching error. God, I do not have a husband who is devoted to me or the children. He lives only for the ministry and I have no say in it anymore. Am I wrong to want him to care more for us?"

My marriage and my ministry had become synonymous. I couldn't possibly dislike something in my marriage because that would reflect badly on the ministry. I didn't dare complain because I had to keep up the image for all of the people who were depending on me. About that time, when we would walk down the aisle to go on the stage, sometimes people would reach out and touch us. That really alarmed me, and I'd get on stage and be sure to tell them, "You have got to look to Jesus for your marriage healing. If Kent and I went out of the ministry, you would have to know that God was telling you to stand. You cannot base your faith on us." (Little did I realize how prophetic a statement I was making.)

It didn't do much good, but I tried. It is easier sometimes to obey rules that people tell you instead of searching out your own relationship with God. Make sure that God is talking to you and that you aren't trying to live off someone else's revelation even though it might be easier.

It seemed I could never satisfy everybody. If I stayed home, I was neglecting the ministry. People would call and say, "Dru, why aren't you supporting your husband by traveling everywhere with him? Meetings are so much better when you are there. The meetings are not complete when you are not ministering together. You are called to be by his side."

I would answer, "I was called to be a mother before I was called to be a minister. I only go to meetings where I know God especially wants me because I can't be a good mother and travel all the time."

Even knowing this was true, condemnation and guilt came all over me. When I traveled, I felt like a rotten mother. I never could find a place of peace. I felt guilty if I stayed home with the girls and guilty when I was on the road. I realize now that I was a performance-oriented person. I thought, "If I'm working as hard and as long as I possibly can, at least God won't find fault with me. I might not do everything perfectly, but God will know I can't work any harder at it, and God can't expect any more out of me than that."

Unconsciously, I was trying to earn God's love.

Where was my joy? Where was my peace? I did not have any. I kept begging God for some answers, "What is wrong? What is wrong?"

One day I was vacuuming my kitchen and relentlessly asking the same old question, "What's wrong, God? Everything looks so good."

My brain didn't calculate the thought, but, all of a sudden, I heard myself cry out of my spirit, "God, I feel like I have started a cult!" Then my head caught up with it, and I said, "Yes, that's how I feel, Lord!"

He spoke to me right then and said, "Dru, you have missed a step."

I don't know if any of you have had this experience but many times God will say very few words to me, but then give me a whole bunch of revelation along with the words. I began to rehearse the steps that I taught people in standing for the healing of their marriage when their partner was gone: Pray and believe in faith that God is healing the marriage; do spirit warfare; confess the Scriptures; intercede in prayer for them; and stand in faith. Then God interjected, "Yes, that is right. Your intercession allows Me to plead My case with those partners who are gone. But I will never transgress their free will. They will have to choose if they want to come home or not. I will never force them, and that is the step that you missed."

Light bulbs went on! That was what I was missing. That was why some marriages didn't get healed.

Just then a friend of mine called to see if I had received the tapes that he had sent me. We had a pile of tapes and books in Kent's office in the basement people had sent us that we could never seem to get through. I decided to try to find these tapes in that pile, and I came up with an envelope of pamphlets written by a Pastor Barnett in Boise, Idaho. He was an assistant pastor in his father's church. There were so many disillusioned "standers" in their church whose marriages had not been healed that his father commissioned him to go over my yellow book with a fine-tooth comb and point out the doctrinal errors. A year and a half before, according to the postmark on the envelope, he had sent me these pamphlets. The first one was on "free will". Considering what God had just said to me, that I missed a step on the free will part, I grabbed that booklet and devoured it. Every bit of it made sense to me! I am sure that I had not opened the pamphlets a year and a half before because I wouldn't have been open-minded enough then to read them or understand what I had read. Then, impulsively, I grabbed the phone and called Boise, Idaho information. I got the pastor's phone number and dialed it. He answered, and I said, "Pastor, this is Dru Axtell," wondering what kind of reception I would get because he really tore my yellow book to shreds.

"Dru Axtell," he said with great joy in his voice, "I have been praying for you for two years!"

I said, "You have? Why?"

He replied, "For you to come out of that bondage."

I told him what had happened and he asked if I had read the rest of the pamphlets.

They all had the same cover so I thought that he had sent me five of the same one. I told him I would call him after I read the other four, and asked if we could discuss them. I had always desired not to teach error, but by now I was certain that I had. Maybe God would give me a chance to correct it.

Pastor Barnett's booklets pointed out that there were people whose faith was literally shipwrecked because their marriage didn't heal. That is why he wrote the pamphlets. He encouraged me to believe that God would make the way for me to correct these errors. I hesitate to think how many thousands were watching us on TBN. I felt such a great responsibility to our viewers. My new friend encouraged me and said that it took a very open-minded person to admit where I was wrong and that God would bless my efforts.

I begged Kent to let me have some space in our newsletter to explain the areas I had been teaching that were wrong. The Standers groups encouraged people to learn all about Jesus. They didn't teach only marriage healing. They had a curriculum where they learned all kinds of things about the Lord in Bible study. Still, in spite of my publicly imploring praying partners not to become "cliff hangers" (that is, to put all their eggs in one basket and feel they can have no happiness unless that partner came home), Standers groups were becoming some of the people's whole identity. Again I say, SOME people, not all, were thinking "I'm a Stander" instead of "I'm a Christian." It may sound rather innocuous and harmless, but it was deception, no matter how subtle. I saw it creeping in to the Standers groups no matter how I preached against it.

Some of the members had wrong motives. Some didn't really love their partner but were afraid to grow old alone or afraid no one else would want them. Some had a holier-than-thou attitude; "I am going teach my mate how wrong he is. I don't love him, but I'm going to show him who is right and pray him home."

Some were martyrs - unconsciously, I'm sure - and afraid to face reality and cope with making a new life for themselves.

Then, too, others were wanting out of their "stand" but, because of my teachings, were afraid that they would be displeasing God if they came off their stand. With all the things that were coming into light for me, I suddenly understood why the pastor in Boise was praying for our ministry to come out of bondage.

Recently, I attended a Bible study at my church with quite a few ladies who were Standers. A word came from the Lord that I took notes on and although this is not verbatim, the general thrust will bring balance to a stand and help check the motive: God said that most people are like Standers or those who want healing. "They have a motive for serving Me." The part that is missing that God desires is to, "Come after Me, seek Me, get so close nothing else makes any difference. Come because you Love Me, not the thing you want.''

I didn't have any Bible college training or teaching. When I wrote the Yellow Book, I was an absolute babe in the Lord. I had no teaching whatsoever except for a few "faith" preachers. I now saw that I had misinterpreted Scriptures left and right and thought everyone who did what I did could get their partner to come home. I had taken my own experience and found Scriptures to back it up.

My friend, Pastor Blix, here in Council Bluffs who counseled me during my time of doctrinal searching taught me about "exogesis" and "isogesis." Exogesis is impartially searching the Scriptures to discover what they truly mean. Isogesis is hunting for scriptures that seem to back up a particular belief.

I can say with all truthfulness that, although I had no idea whatsoever it was a wrong approach, most of my writings were composed by doing the latter.

I searched methodically for hours and hours for Scriptures to back up my belief that ALL marriages could be healed and ignored any that seemed to contradict my zealous ideal.

Consequently, we were not accepted in many churches who thought we were kookier than a three dollar bill! I now understand, of course, but...we sure did get a lot of marriages healed that others were afraid to tackle. I thank God for blessing our sincere efforts and desires to see every marriage healed in spite of our misguided doctrines. But I can't ignore the errors once I know them. It's not the healed marriages I write this for... it's for all those who tried to stand and didn't get it who are still blaming themselves for their failure or for not having a strong enough faith.

If only I'd seen the balance sooner. Each person must go before God until he or she is certain God is telling them to stand in faith for their partner to come home. Every person must let God direct them step by step individually, not build their belief on someone else's miracle. Testimonies of miracles tell what God can do for a person. They do not guarantee He will do likewise for everyone. Read Paul's summation after his instructions about marriage and divorce in I Corinthians 7:17 in the Amplified version: "Only, let each one [seek to conduct himself and regulate his affairs so as to] lead the life which the Lord has allotted and imparted to him and to which God has invited and summoned him. This is my order in all the churches."

My whole Christian walk began with Kent when he came home. He heard a voice which we both assumed was the Holy Spirit speaking a message to him when we would sit down and pray in the Spirit together about a particular problem that we had. Some of those messages are recorded in the Yellow Book and we taught them like they were Gospel. I also got into the submission teaching that a wife's whole duty was to submit to her husband, even if he asked her to do something sinful. As long as her will was submitted to God and to her husband, God would make a way out of the sinful situation. If her husband insisted that she go to a wife-swapping party, she should say, "Well, all right, dear. I don't want to go but whatever you say." Then she would run to her prayer closet and cry to God, "God, get me out of this," and He would. How could I or any other wife be so blind?

Actually, I do know some of the answers. Let me quote from an article in the June issue of *Glamour* magazine about abused women. This is by a daughter being sexually abused by her father. Her mother would comfort her afterwards but never say anything about it. The daughter "couldn't put her awful secret into words, and her mother could never allow herself to know it consciously. That would have meant standing up for herself and her daughter, rejecting or punishing her husband - destroying the myth of the happy, loving family that gave her a place and a function. Facing facts would have deprived her of the man on whom she depended completely."

I've never been physically abused in any way, thank God, but I empathized with the wife in the article. Those are most of the reasons I refused to consciously admit the fallacies of the "wife submit to all" doctrine and chose not to stand my ground when it came to charging and borrowing and anything else I didn't approve of. Other reasons came later with the growth of the ministry. I didn't want to let people down who loved us and depended on us to minister to them and be their "standard" for a healed marriage. Most of all, I had grown so totally dependent on Kent for everything that fear would come over me at the thought of refusing to obey him to the point of losing the only way of life I knew. I never felt secure throughout our marriage, but I was familiar with the insecurity.

Not only did I bite my lip and put my own ideals and innate wisdom aside but also my own common good sense! We could preach that we never fought because if what I felt was right conflicted with what Kent wanted, I just let it go.

The "message" came early in our reconciliation that I was never to mention a problem with Kent and he was never to mention a problem with me to any other person. God alone would be our Counselor. That bizarre message controlled us from then on. I was too unsure of myself to question the validity of it, and Kent never questioned whether he was hearing from God. This gave the devil ground to make us do some strange things - all for Jesus, of course. And we had no outsider to ask for wisdom or another opinion.

But at the time I prayed Kent home and made the vow to bow to his every wish to insure he would stay home, I had no way of knowing the misery years of living that way would cause me.

A concerned friend wondered if I was writing this book out of my own hurt. To that I answered, "Definitely not!" It hurts too badly to be this open about all our private life. In myself, I'd rather keep quiet about all my embarrassing failures, but I cannot before God.

In the months that I spent at home while the ministry gradually closed down feeling like a total failure and just wanting to fade into oblivion somewhere - friends and pastors kept calling me urging me to write what I had learned. And finally, God began to wake me morning after morning with the urgency to write in the middle of my crisis.

In checking out my doctrinal errors with pastors I knew around the country, I had discovered I was not the only ministry wife living under the "submit to your husband in all things" deception. I learned of churches preaching this cultish doctrine to the extent that if anything went wrong, the wives of the pastors and leaders of the churches were blamed. "They must be out of submission somewhere." I personally know of pastors' wives having nervous breakdowns because of this type of burden placed on them. Others, like me - when Kent and I finally went for counseling - felt **dead** on the inside from putting their own personality aside for so long. One pastor's wife in Omaha who used to be a spirited, bubbly Christian is a walking zombie in and out of mental institutions because although she doesn't know how, for sure, but her husband assured her their church closed because she wasn't submitting to him enough.

Ephesians 5:21 says to "Submit to one another..." Verse 25 says, "Husbands, love your wives, just as Christ loved the church and gave himself up for her." I Peter 3:7 says to "be considerate...treat them with respect...so that nothing will hinder your prayers." (NIV)

I would like to quote from *Thoroughly Married*, by Dr. Dennis Guernsey.

> "The words and situations change from couple to couple but the issue remains the same. A wife is to do as she is told whether she likes it or not. Some commands come in the form of quiet orders. Others come in the form of bellowed ultimatums. What is consistent is that the husband always has the last word. The wife must always do as she is told.
>
> "I think that this approach is inconsistent with the will of God because it isn't biblical. Why do I say this? Because the ex-submission has been modeled for us in the relationship between the Son and the Father.
>
> "We are told in the Scriptures that Jesus was submissive to His Father in everything, (John 17:4) and His submission was voluntary. Never was He coerced to do anything. Had He been forced to do the will of the Father, His response would have been meaningless. By application, if a wife is to

submit to her husband she is to do so voluntarily. Even when he feels strongly about an issue he must give her the freedom to make up her own mind and not try to make it up for her.

"What makes this kind of relationship difficult is that the husband must give up his absolute power. He can no longer dictate. He must negotiate. In giving up his absolute control over his wife he gains something in return, the voluntary acquiescence of a willing partner. She is free to be herself and free to respond."

For me to consider the above mentioned Scriptures or views might actually apply to me is almost shocking. I certainly never preached them. I was too busy submitting! I didn't think I could ask for any of these to be considered.

However, anything under pressure will finally explode and I did. Now I can see why Peter and Paul commanded us to live Godly lives, not submitting to anything we think is wrong. Wives are to submit to their husbands "as to the Lord" (Eph. 5:22). The Lord would never ask us to do anything wrong or put burdens on us we could not handle. Jesus said in Matthew 11:30, "For my yoke is easy, and my burden is light." (KJV)

Did you know that they carved each ox's yoke to fit his neck or it would rub raw spots? If your "yoke" for Jesus is driving you to distraction, better find out who put the yoke on you.

Husbands, if you feel conviction that you've blatantly or subtly lorded the submission doctrine over your wife and she might be ready to explode - or maybe she's hinted she's about to leave you, it's not too late! Ask her forgiveness humbly and decide to **work together** for a healthy, vibrant TWO-WAY marriage.

Also, husbands reading this who are getting angry, this is probably a warning to you. Your wife wasn't given to you by God to serve as a brainless slave. God does not put the institution of marriage above the sanity of one of His precious daughters.

When Kent would go on ministry trips for a week at a time, I was expected to take care of the girls, run the house, make ministry decisions, and handle angry bill collectors. When he came home, if I forgot my place and was too enthusiastic or opinionated about something I was told that I was too strong-willed and trying to run things.

I remember one instance specifically when I wanted to go shopping. After questioning me as to why I had to go that day, he then told me what street to drive on. A sense of frustration came over me, and I turned and said, "Why do you ever leave me alone with the children if I can't make a simple decision like this? I just cannot seem to remember to shut my brain off the minute you walk back in the door!"

Then I repented for such an independent outburst.

It's a miracle I didn't have one of those "outbursts" right on stage or on television as I began to decipher what was hypocrisy and wrong doctrine and just tell everything to everybody publicly. I wanted to but I had curbed myself too long. I had thought it was God wanting me to live this submitted life for so many years, I could not come free easily.

It has been almost two years since God spoke to me concerning free will. It has taken all that time for me to get brave enough to refuse to keep quiet, stand for what I know to be true and do what I had to do in order to set the record straight for any person I may have harmfully influenced. I am trusting God to see that those persons read this book.

Taping "Marriage on the Rock"
in Patti and Gavin's Santa Monica apartment.

Filming "Marriage on the Rock" with
Shirley and Pat Boone by their pool.

10

DISCOVERING ERROR

The night I got saved I prayed that God would bring Kent home even though Kent did not want to come home.

The understanding that I had as a baby Christian was that if we prayed in faith, believing, because the Scripture says that it is God's most perfect will that marriages not end in divorce, then God had to answer the prayer. I learned to bind the devil in Jesus name. I would speak to whatever spirits seemed to be obviously operating in the person's life such as alcohol, adultery, lust, or whatever and forbid their activity in the name of Jesus. I thought if we stopped the voices of whatever spirits were influencing that person, then our prayer intercession would allow God to talk to that person and urge him to come home. I taught everyone to do as I had done totally ignoring the person's free will. I had read in Romans 7 where there is the "will of the flesh" and the "will of the spirit." So I thought if we bound up the devils that were influencing the "will of the flesh," then the husband or wife could hear God telling him or her to come home and the "will of the spirit," if they were saved, would win over the "will of the flesh." I am not saying that it can't ever happen that way because I've seen it work too many times. I was missing it by believing that since it happened to Kent that way, it was a guaranteed doctrine or a formula. If you do A, B and C, God will work for you. I took the faith teaching to mean whatever you say is what you are going to get, regardless of sin, circumstances, free will, or whatever else was in the way.

When Kent did come home, he always said that he came home against his will. He told God that he didn't want to come home to me but God had said that he should go home. So he said, "Okay, God, I am going to obey You instead of doing what I want."

I tried to figure that out doctrinally. I concluded that the "will of his flesh" didn't want to, but his love for God made the "will of his spirit" take over and his spirit man wanted to obey God. I knew that God didn't exactly force him. He returned home because he wanted to please God and believed, as I did, that God would heal everything between us. But I believed and taught that God would woo and love that person into **choosing** to come home no matter how long it took. I believe you didn't have to give free will a thought because once a person became acquainted personally with the majesty of Jesus Christ, who could resist Him?

If Kent had said, "No, God. I am going to do it my way no matter what You say to me," God would have allowed him not to come home. I didn't know that. I thought God would just keep on working on him until he gave in so to speak. I knew how much Kent wanted to marry another girl, and I thought, "Nobody's free will can get any stronger than Kent's but God handled him and sent him home!" I reasoned that if God did that with Kent, He would do the same for anyone else who prayed and waited patiently for God's timing!

Because of this, we taught that all marriages could be healed if one spouse stood in faith for as long as it took - no matter what happened. Now I see that there are so many doctrines out that are built on one person's revelation. I got a gift of faith to pray Kent home the minute I got saved. Understand that I was almost an atheist when I gave my heart to Jesus. In a split second, legally I was a full-blooded daughter of the King but that didn't mean I had any sound biblical knowledge. What happened when I prayed for Kent to come home overwhelmed me. I'm sure God gave me a gift of faith. It didn't matter how bad it looked; Kent was coming home. I never wavered, no one could talk me out of it. No one could bring me down from the rosy cloud. I knew that I knew that I knew. And, sure enough, he came home! So I began teaching everyone to do exactly as I had done without any Bible teaching other than whatever tapes I chose to listen to or faith books or my own Bible study.

A great portion of the people we shared with **did** get their marriages healed just as I did. Of course, many didn't. For a long time we explained it away thinking they had given up on their faith too soon.

I thought that God had given me that kind of revelation and had done that miracle so I would have a message for people in the same kind of trouble. I didn't have the least idea that I shouldn't share my personal revelation as though everyone could have it unconditionally! So I taught that if anybody would stand and believe in faith, not weaken under contrary-looking circumstances - even remarriage by the spouse - just hang in there long enough, God would bring their partner home. After all, hadn't Kent come in to the beauty salon where I worked and bought cosmetics from me for his girlfriend? How much more discouraging could it have looked?

In the meantime, we told them not to sit around and pine away for that partner. They had to get to know Jesus and truly live for Him, and thank God, that will always be good preaching. We turned people who had been left by their spouses from emotional basket cases into... "Standers". Some pastors said, "Your 'Standers' are the best members that I've got. They know how to pray. They love Jesus and want to serve Him. Anytime I need some help, I can always count on the 'Standers'." And that was the intent of the Standers groups - to help people through the crisis stage and into becoming healthy, dynamic Christians while waiting for their marriage to be healed.

We saw so many people sincerely wanting to serve the Lord, on their knees before God, saying, "Do something with me, Lord. Show me what is wrong and where my faults are. Make me into a Godly (husband or wife)."

But on the negative side, I began to see that many were simply afraid to go out in the world and seek a new life. They chose to be a "Stander" the rest of their life. This was their "cross to bear", their identity. I saw many continue to feel frustration and pain but at least the pain was familiar to them, and sometimes it is easier to cope with familiar pain than to launch off into the unknown, especially if you think God wants you there, even though God may have blessings and freedom just waiting around the corner if they would tune in HIM instead of the group mind-set!

I felt so bad for those people, and I didn't know what to do about it. For many years I didn't know myself that God would ever tell someone, "Your stand is over. You have stood long enough." I thought that that was giving up.

As our ministry progressed, we began to see marriage healings in every kind of situation that you could imagine. In the early years, I thought that every marriage healing would manifest like Kent's and mine. He had filed for a divorce, but God brought him home before the divorce was final. Our lawyer did not even send us a bill because he was so happy that we had gotten back together again. But then in some situations where the praying partner seemed to have mountain-moving faith, the divorce would go through. The first time this happened, we got on our knees before God and asked, "What about this, God?"

He said, "Stand and watch."

People in the world break up, get divorced, and decide that it was wrong, and get remarried. So we would wait those out. That seemed to prove that if you stand long enough, you are going to get your healing eventually. We took God's word on this one individual marriage to be true for any other praying person's marriage when the divorce became legal.

Sometimes a partner would leave, get a divorce, have a girlfriend or a boyfriend, and even marry the partner of that affair. The first partner would just hang in there with all the faith in the world, and we would actually see that second marriage crumble and end in divorce. There would, then, be a remarriage. This was not an every day event, but it happened often enough that people would ask, "How can that be?"

Deuteronomy 24:1-4 says, "When a man hath taken a wife, and married her, and it come to pass that she find no favour in his eyes... let him write her a bill of divorcement, and give it in her hand and send her out of his house. And when she is departed out of his house, she may go and be another man's wife. And if the latter husband hate her, and write her a bill of divorcement... her former husband, which sent her away, may not take her again to his wife..."

I put a lot of study into that portion of Scripture, concluding that in those days, men were taking advantage of the divorce provision, sort of legalizing their adultery. They would divorce their wife so they could have an affair, and when it was over they many times planned on remarrying their first partner because they didn't want to get stoned for the adultery a momentary "fling" would create for them. So God, through Moses, put an end to that little game. I still believe that the divorce clause in Deuteronomy 24 contained protection for wives in that patriarchal society. We figured that didn't have anything to do with New Testament law, and besides, the civil authority of our land allows this kind of remarriage. It is almost funny how you can "legalistically" make the Bible say whatever you want.

People who were against our ministry used Deuteronomy 24:1-4 to say unequivocally remarriage to a former partner was wrong. Yet we see it happen so many times, I'm sure God in His grace judges the individual circumstance. Just as I now believe it is wrong to make a blanket doctrine out of that one Scripture, it was wrong for me to make a doctrine which said, "Keep on standing. If your partner remarries, it **will** crumble, and you **will** get your partner back if you just keep on standing in faith. Don't be discouraged by the remarriage."

By the time I realized I was wrong and couldn't make a blanket promise like that and took the chapter out of my yellow book, I couldn't stop the flood of people with remarried partners who wanted to believe it and refused not to. They just took old copies and reprinted them and continued giving it to friends in similar situations.

God does tell people when they have stood long enough and should get on with their life. However, for years I thought that they were motivated by doubt and disbelief. God certainly tells people who are praying and spending time with Him, when to keep on standing, and that was all I knew about.

If a partner used abusive language, I would tell the one praying to write down everything the other had said that is absolutely against Scripture and we would come against it by binding the devil. This happened in one of the first marriages that I ever counseled. Instead of the wife being crushed by her husband's words, she would sit there with her pen and paper and write down every ungodly thing that he said. The next day we would come against it verbatim and bind the spirits influencing him in Jesus' name. Oddly enough, he wouldn't say those same phrases anymore. He would say something different. Then we would bind the devil again. It worked. After a while he didn't speak abusively and they dated again. After about two years, he was born again. They were remarried and stayed happily married for twelve more years until he passed on to be with the Lord.

Because of that experience, I started doing that with everybody, but it didn't always give such effective results. People would ask, "How many times a day do I have to bind this stuff to get it to work?"

I would say, "Ask God," all the while wondering the same thing myself.

I still don't have all the answers as to why binding and loosing worked so well in some cases and not at all in others. We know Jesus didn't always heal all the sick people He came in contact with and said He only did what His Father told Him to do. Perhaps binding gets noticeable results when it is a Holy Spirit inspired instruction for a specific instance.

In one instance, a lady's husband said to her, "I am leaving town today. I am never coming back. And I will never set my foot in this house again."

She called me. We prayed and bound up his truck from starting. Are you ready for this? His truck would not start. Later on, after he got it fixed, my daughter was babysitting his kids when he drove his truck right up onto the front yard and stormed through the front door. After that we had more ammunition to teach that whatever spirits we bind are inoperative. That marriage did get healed for a while but later on fell apart again.

When a distraught, heartbroken person called me and wanted to know what to do when their partner had just done something that wounded them deeply, it seemed healthier and more productive to me to pray the prayer of binding and loosing than to sit there and cry all night.

But recently, I saw it begin to evolve into almost witchcraft. I really became alarmed when my daughter was staying in the home of a "Stander". They had a prayer meeting, and one woman's husband had remarried. She was afraid if there were children born into that union that he would never come home so they "cursed" the second wife's womb. They were also praying that if she got pregnant, the baby would die. My daughter called me and said, "Mother, get me out of here! They are binding wombs and praying that babies die."

Ladies I were personally acquainted with began coming to me and confessing they'd been praying that way and GOD had told them it was wrong so they had repented and wanted me to know that it was wrong.

I was stunned and thought, "Dear God, what have I started? We didn't personally teach that but it is happening in our ministry and it has got to stop.

These are dear, sweet people but they have gotten into a mind-set of, "I am going to get my husband back, bless God, no matter what it takes!" instead of, "I'm going to serve Jesus with my life, and if it's His will for my partner to come back, then it's icing on the cake."

This is one of my passions for writing this book. These dear people have got to realize that this type of "praying" is not spirit warfare but tantamount to witchcraft. I have checked this with many preachers and evangelists from coast to coast, and they ALL agree: This is witchcraft, and no Christian should participate in it.

Another fact people must realize is that some marriages will not get healed. Some are going to have to pick up the pieces of their life and, with God's help, start over.

In our ministry, we seemed to have lost sight of God's having control and being able to say, "I am giving you revelation knowledge. Your marriage IS going to be healed," or realizing God could also say, "You have stood and prayed long enough. I am sending you a husband or wife who wants to serve God with you."

In the ministry, I met a hodgepodge of Christians. Some people I got acquainted with have every virtue of faith and love God with all their heart. They pray, fast, and read their Bible. To my knowledge they don't have any great sins in their life. They truly love that partner who is gone, and they are trusting God to send that partner home. I have watched them wait six, eight, ten years - and nothing!

On the other hand, I've watched others pray, act like a basket case, not read their Bible, cry on everybody's shoulder, and rely on everybody else's faith. They would even go out on dates, and yet their partner would come home in three months. Their marriage was healed, but they didn't do anything "right". It used to boggle my mind.

When God opened my eyes to free will, it was an answer to an awful lot of questions. I couldn't wait. I wanted to communicate this to all of the "Standers". At all of our conventions people hung on every word that I said because I was the original "Stander". I had stood in faith and prayed my partner home when he didn't want to come home. Every time I thought I had a revelation from God, I would write another chapter and add it to the "Yellow" book to communicate with all the Standers. I would always share anything I learned either in my writing or public speaking.

The "Yellow" book used to have different kinds of type in it because every chapter might have been done on a different typewriter at a different time.

When I knew for certain I'd taught some wrong doctrines, I felt I owed it to all the people involved in our ministry, if I cared about them, to admit where I was wrong and teach correct doctrine. I asked Kent to let me share my new knowledge about my doctrinal errors with all the people on our mailing list and at our meetings, but he said, "No, we will lose them all. How in the world would they ever stand? Give me some time to catch up with what you **think** you know. Write it all down, and I will study it."

I told him, "I don't have to do that. It is already in some pamphlets a pastor sent me. Please, read them."

This went on for months. I couldn't get my husband to take the time to read the pamphlets. I so badly wanted Kent to read them and see if he agreed with them. If he did, then we could teach the various "Stander" groups the correct doctrines. I wanted to bring balance to our ministry and get rid of error and bondage.

Every doctrine that I know of - faith, healing, discipleship, binding and loosing, and prosperity - originated with someone who received a personal revelation on a certain Scripture from God and preached it many times to the exclusion of other balancing scriptures in the Bible.

My friend, Pastor Blix, here in Council Bluffs, said to me one day, "Dru, there are two kinds of churches. Some preach the Cross of Christ and His suffering, and some preach the glory walk. Which do you think is right?"

I thought a moment and replied, "Well, I think they are both right."

He said, "That's absolutely correct. But most churches tend to preach all one way or the other. Suffering all the way or glory all the way. Churches should teach that both are included in the Christian life.

We did the same thing. I got my revelation. It worked for me. And I taught it to the exclusion of balancing scriptures. "If you do what I did, you can get what I got."

I completely misinterpreted "God is no respecter of persons" to mean everyone who follows the formula can get the same thing. The bad part of it for me was that when I was thrust before the public eye, I was afraid it would be more then people's faith could handle if I said, "Your healing might take place right away or it might be six years, twelve years, or even twenty years down the road. Then again, it may never happen, God only knows. Pray 'til you find out.'' I really felt it would descredit God if I dared to admit I didn't have all my healing yet, for which I believed God, but I was stuck with it because I was in the limelight. I was up there as an image. I didn't dare get on the stage and say, "I can hardly have sex with my husband," because we were preaching that we had a happy marriage. That was the cross that I was bearing, and they may have to bear a few too if they prayed their partner home against his will.

I wasn't about to say that because it wasn't faith, and besides, I didn't want to hurt anyone. I was accustomed to swallowing the hurt myself instead of making someone else hurt. Now I wonder how many people were hurt and disillusioned by my misunderstanding of living by faith.

A lot of physical illnesses come from trying to look so great on the outside and be what people expect us to be as "representatives" of Christ. That is a noble motive, but as leaders, we then don't have anyone to go to and say, "Help! I have this huge problem. I am up here representing God as a marriage healer, but I still have marriage problems!"

People don't think that leaders should have any problems. I didn't think we were **allowed** to have any problems! Well, we've got them! The time is here that we start living in truth before God and the people we serve and admit our shortcomings and expect leaders to have counselors too!

Proverbs 11:14 says, "Where no counsel is, the people fall: but in the multitude of counselors there is safety." When that message came to Kent that we weren't to have any counselors, I used to wonder, "But what about Proverbs 11:24?"

We were "special". Our circumstance called for different rules. Now I realize we were not only deceived but also it was pride to think we had it so together, that we never needed to counsel with other older and wiser members of the body of Christ. Ultimately, we see where there was no counsel the ministry fell.

After a year or so I asked Kent once again to allow me to tell what I had learned and he still refused.

It hurt me that their support came before telling them the

truth. In no submissive way, I said that the "ministry" was not some inanimate object. It was individual people who have problems and souls that need ministry and deserve to hear the truth once I finally learn it. They were not a big mass that supplied money for us. The ministry was my bread and butter, too, but I preferred to tell the truth and go into secular work than to tickle their ears with what some wanted to hear to keep the money coming in. God help us!

Me and Peter, my son-in-law.

Illustrates all of us looking good on stage,
girls and me in silk dresses, etc.

My friend, Rita Hunt and Gavin at his
wedding reception.

11

OUR MARRIAGE
IN TROUBLE

After reading the pamphlets on "free will", I began to call pastors and evangelists all across the country who had well-known, sound ministries. I told them about God telling me that I had missed a step, and I would ask them, "Is that why you didn't support our ministry? I know that you loved us personally."

Their response was "Yes, Dru. Now you are right on."

Others who did support our ministry said, "I knew all the time you were out of balance in that area, but I helped our people eat the meat and spit out the bones because we loved you and thought that it was a noble cause. You did give the divorced people who were basket cases a reason to live and learn about Jesus."

Another said, "That is why I didn't let my church become involved with you wholeheartedly and back you up with our name. But I didn't come against you publicly because it was wonderful to see whatever marriages could be healed."

I made call after call, from coast to coast, and had

enough witnesses tell me that I now had correct understanding in the "free will" area. I felt sure that I should communicate it to all of the "Standers".

At the same time, my oldest daughter, Kristin, had left home to attend Victory Bible Institute in Tulsa. Peter, her fiance, was attending Oral Roberts University to get a Bachelor of Arts degree in Theology with emphasis on the New Testament.

Peter had to write a thesis, and he chose the subject, "Divorce and Remarriage in the New Testament".

Peter and Kristin were both loyal supporters of Born Again Marriages. Kristin had grown up on the front pew of many churches watching her parents preach. She could counsel distraught people on how to stand for the healing of their marriage as well as I could from the time she was eight years old.

Peter came from a broken home and hoped to minister to children from broken homes through our ministry some day. He had worked in our ministry three summers.

As they began to study together for Peter's thesis, it came as no small shock to them when their searching the Scriptures revealed they did not agree at all with what Kent and I taught!

Imagine the situation. I was at home wondering if Peter and Kristin would regard me as a "traitor to the cause" if I told them I felt I'd been preaching some wrong doctrines and there was error in our ministry.

Kristin and Peter were in Tulsa fretting over how to break it to me that they were no longer in agreement with what we preached or what I had written in my book.

We talked often, and as I broached the subject cautiously, what a relief to the three of us to find out that, totally independent of one another, we'd discovered the same truths! Not only was there no split because of doctrinal differences which we'd all feared, but we were closer than ever because we could openly discuss everything. The three of us spent hours on the phone. We felt sort of like brand-new Christians as the light flooded in while we shared together.

Peter and Kristin adamantly agreed that I needed to level

with the Standers. They felt as I did that anyone who had revelation from God that their marriage would be healed would not be harmed by the truth, and those who were making "standing" their god would be freed from this bondage.

Kristin and Peter were getting married in June of 1987. I tried to hold my peace when I realized that Kent and I were at such odds with each other. Instead, I devoted myself to putting my daughter's wedding together. I didn't want anything to spoil her joy. Little did I know that "they knew very well that they were sitting on a powder keg," as my son-in-law said later. My usual role of being the silent martyr had not paid off at all.

At this time we had about twenty-five people working for our ministry, and the money was not coming in. I was not going to the office very much because I couldn't stand the growing debt of the ministry since I could do nothing about it. At our annual convention an evangelist that had come to speak prophesied over the ministry that if we didn't become better stewards of God's money that God would remove the anointing from the ministry in ninety days. Kent repented then and there. I thought, "Thank God, I'm not crazy."

Kent began to counsel with our pastor and another pastor who had been a friend from the time we were saved. I felt that between the two of them, ministry spending would stop, and maybe we would come out of this. The fact that I felt dead inside frightened me more than anything. Spending habits could be corrected, but what about the horrible numbness I felt on the inside?

Our pastor even agreed to take our ministry under the auspices of his church and help with the debts. Both these men loved us dearly and devoted time and energy to counseling us. I was so grateful to them.

The ministry had not paid the employee withholding tax again and ended up in debt to the IRS. We had to sell our office building to pay what we owed the government. I feared I was seeing the beginning of the end. I wept until I couldn't quit. My mind was telling me to stop but it was coming from my insides like water through a dam that had burst. Our office had been a gift from God, and through our negligence, we had lost it.

Kent decided a few months later that the evangelist was wrong and said the period of repentance was over. He said there couldn't be a lot of heads to the ministry, and he was THE head. He stopped all of the counseling with our two pastors and asked a lady in the ministry who had college training in business administration to come and straighten out the ministry financially. I remarked I didn't need a college education to know you don't spend money you don't have.

I asked her not to come because I was afraid God was removing the anointing from the ministry and funds would drop so low that she probably wouldn't get a paycheck. She assured me that with her training and experience she could get a job anywhere if we couldn't pay her, but our ministry was her mission in life. I gave up trying to convince her not to come.

Kent never took the time to read the pamphlets concerning our doctrinal errors. He had decided that I had totally backslidden because I could no longer sit on the stage with a plastic smile. I told him I didn't have a husband and the kids didn't have a father because he was out telling everyone else how to be good husbands and fathers and was never home. I insisted we had to live what we preached or resign. He started taping the television show without me because what I felt was showing on my face.

Kent would say to me, "We have a calling on our life. Shape up and get with the program. You can't back out on God."

This didn't fix the hurts on the inside. I couldn't believe that he could go on and pretend that everything was okay. I asked him, "How do you think that you can go out and preach how to have a happy marriage when you have a wife at home who is telling you that she is miserable?"

"Preachers who are physically sick are still preaching physical healing. I can't stop preaching because we have problems. This is my call in life," he responded.

The woman who came to straighten out the ministry had received a personal prophecy that she was sent to replace me in the ministry while I was in my backslidden condition. Kent rented another office. I was vice-president of the ministry, but I wasn't given a key to the front door of the new office because, I guess, now I was the enemy. I appeared to be coming against my own ministry. I truly had no thought of doing such a thing. I only wanted the people delivered out of bondage and untruth!

One day Kent came home and told me that all the employees had quit. He was pleased because they were all in rebellion, and now the slate was clean, so he could start all over. I named names of loyal people who had been with us in the basement of our home where the ministry started. I absolutely couldn't imagine that they would just quit.

I attended a wedding of a former employee right after that and saw the girl who headed our letter writing department whom I'd been very close to and asked, "Why did you quit, Carol? Can you tell me why?"

She looked a little startled and said, "Dru, I think we should have lunch."

We did, the next day and I discovered that Kent had come into the office and said, "Dru and I had a long prayer session, and it is our mutual agreement that you should all quit." It seems none of the ministry employees believed the lady's prophecy was of God and were not in agreement with it. Also the ministry finances were down so they were told they were "laid off".

I didn't know a thing about it! All of this was showing our growing weakness in the area of honesty and agreement with your partner that we preached the loudest and strongest. We taught that if we built our marriage upon the Rock (Jesus), storms could come against us, even floods, and we would still stand on the Rock. I thought that our marriage was founded on the Rock. However, when the big storm hit, it crumbled. Though our intentions were good, we were standing on the "sand" of doctrinal error and being deceptive from the start. Understand I know very well I was the one who did not level with Kent from the beginning of our marriage. Somehow, we managed to get through Kristin and Peter's wedding. It was the loveliest wedding I had ever seen.

Kristin and Peter wrote out their own vows and it was thrilling to see the love radiating from their faces as they spoke them to each other. It was a picture-book wedding from start to finish.

After their honeymoon Kristin opened up to me and said, "Mom, I have never been real happy because I haven't had a father. He has always been gone. I always felt the ministry stole my father."

She told me that she had asked her dad when she knew that the month before the wedding, she was leaving home forever, "Please stay home this month," with tears running down her face.

He said, "I can't do that."

That's when she realized how the ministry meant everything to her father.

I knew none of this. I thought that my kids didn't know any other way of life. It certainly wasn't how I'd grown up, but, as usual, I was trying to be a martyr and live with it, and I thought that they were happy. At least they had a father, their parents were together, and we certainly had other pleasures in life.

We wept together, and I said to Kristin, "I'm sorry. I thought that I was sheltering you. I thought that I was doing the right thing."

Soon after this I went grocery shopping with my youngest daughter Mandy, nine-years-old. She burst out crying and told me, "Mom, I don't have anyone to talk to. There's something wrong, and no one will tell me anything. I feel so trapped like we are all just waiting to see what dad is going to do. They are talking awful funny down at the office, and I thought I was the only one who noticed."

I hugged her and said, "I'm so sorry. You can talk to me and tell me anything you want. We won't try to shelter each other anymore. You can tell me anything that bothers you any time." And we cried together there in the middle of the grocery store parking lot.

With the suddenness of a summer storm, my girls and I were leveling with one another.

I began telling Kent, "I really resent your being on the

phone with ministry people every minute that you are in the house." He would say, "Get the resentment out of your heart. That is not God."

I tried to explain to Kent that our kids hadn't been happy and felt neglected. I said, "Kent, you know better than anyone that God formed the family unit before He ever formed ministries. You need to spend more time with Mandy."

A week or so later this was illustrated for us in neon lights. Kent had been gone for three nights and four days, ministering. Mandy went with me to the airport to get him. He got in the car and said something like, "It's good to be back."

Mandy off-handedly said, "I didn't even know you were gone, Dad."

After years of living for my family and my ministry, all my mistakes seemed to be coming to fruition in front of my very eyes.

Howard McCrary and me in my kitchen.

T.B.N. equipment filming our show.

12

"DRU, IT'S OVER!"

Feeling convinced that marriage is made up of mutual cooperation, I could no longer be a doormat. For so many years I thought that God would be mad at me if I stood up to Kent in any way. I believed my mission in life from God was to fulfill Kent's every need. But I had come to the point where I simply prayed, "God, if I foul it up, You are just going to have to forgive me. I am out here treading on brand new territory. I don't know what is wrong or right about submitting. All I know is that I can't live the way I have been any longer. If I really mess it up, I beg You to forgive me."

After Kristin's wedding, things seemed to catapult to a final crisis. I had dug in my heels and said, "Kent, I'm not going a step further unless there are some changes made. This isn't right before God! If we have to shut the ministry down for a while and go to work, we need to pay all the people we owe and be respectable."

I asked him to take the Yellow Book off the market even though it wasn't all wrong. I wasn't worried about the people whose marriages had been healed. I was worried about those whose faith was being shipwrecked.

Kent said, "Rewrite the Yellow Book."

I was in such inner turmoil that I couldn't write. I was too upset. My marriage and ministry seemed to be crumbling before my eyes, but I just could not compromise my ideals or adjust to Kent's every whim and demand any longer... even to save the roof over my head.

During the time we went to our two pastors for counseling, I took their advice and told Kent all the truth from the start of our relationship. When Kent left the room for a phone call, I broke down, cried, and said to one pastor, "I am afraid to go home because I've told him all of the truth, that I married him to get a ticket out of town. I know I have hurt him but he's been quoting the Scriptures to prove that I'm defrauding him if I don't meet his demands. I can't do it right now, and I'm afraid."

I believe this statement by Dr. Dennis Guernsey in *Thoroughly Married* is where I was at:

> A woman's respect for her husband magnifies her ability to respond to him sexually consistently over time. If she doesn't respect him on rare occasions she can conjure up some kind of sexual response through a combination of fantasy and because it's the right time of the month and her hormones are cooperating. But the real test comes at the other times of the month, when she may not "feel" as sexy. At those times she needs more than her raw instincts. She needs someone she "wants" to respond to, someone she "wants" to please. It becomes difficult to respond to someone for whom she feels disgust or disrespect.

When Kent came back in the room, my pastor told Kent, "Your wife is afraid to go home with you. She doesn't feel able to make love with you at this time so you are going to have to fast from sex for a while. She can't handle it, and it isn't right that you pressure her. She stood for you. Now you stand for her."

I felt sure Kent would "stand" for me because of what he preached. I was scared to death that he would stand, and yet perhaps I would stay dead on the inside. What would I do then? I could no longer fake it.

I didn't have long to worry because his stand lasted about a month. During that time he began to fix things around the house if I mentioned that something was broken. He mowed the lawn without my asking him. He tried to come home early and be with Mandy and me.

I would always thank him, but I wasn't convinced it was a heart change. I waited to see if it lasted or if it was merely to get me back into my old role again, quit "rebelling", and be the submissive wife once more.

I do not say this to exonerate myself. I don't know if what I did was totally right. I only know that at the time I didn't have the will to do otherwise. Part of me was dead, and part of me was so tired and disillusioned.

Kent began to travel on ministry trips and not give me a phone number. He might mutter what state he was going to, possibly even the city, but he would not give me the phone number. I felt that I was being treated like I wasn't a worthwhile enough person to be told where to contact him, even in case of an emergency. I have to admit that it was hard. I had to fight the resentment and anger. This went on for several months, but it felt like years. I knew that he knew we certainly didn't preach it was okay to act this way.

I began to feel he was trying to force me into getting back in line or into getting a divorce. I wasn't sure which. I had seen it down through the years: a partner would begin to act so intolerable at home that the other partner would finally be forced into getting out. I marveled that he could still go on stage and preach sanctity of the home and marriage healing. My respect level went to zero.

The final blow came after he said that he was going to California. California is a big state. I wouldn't have known where to call him if I had desperately needed him. Four days later he came home, driving his father's car and carrying a jug of cider so I knew that he had been to his parent's. I said, "How did you get from California to your father's?"

He said, "I've been there the last two days."

Something snapped. I thought, "What if I had had an emergency? I wouldn't have known where to get him. I thought he was in California. Instead, he was thirty miles away!"

I decided to test him and see if he was trying to force me into a divorce. I put Mandy to bed and prayed in the Spirit to calm myself so that I would not blow my stack. By now I knew that whenever I came apart and yelled, he turned a deaf ear to me. I went out and calmly said, "I give up. You win. I will give you a nice, quiet divorce. All I ask is that you please help me keep the house so that we don't have to upset Mandy's way of life any more than necessary."

I don't know how to judge myself for this act. It was against everything that I believed in but felling at the breaking point I had decided to find out if this was what he wanted. Now I feel I know what people mean when they say, "God forgives you for choosing the lesser of the evils."

Very calmly, like he had already thought it out, Kent agreed and said that he thought it was a good idea. He told me he would help me keep the house. He told me to go see a lawyer the next day. I went to bed, and he went to the basement. Mercifully, sleep came.

The next day I prepared to go see the lawyer. Kent came upstairs crying and sobbing saying that God had awakened him and had taken the blinders off, and we needed to talk. I took Mandy to school and came home about 8:30 in the morning. We talked and cried till about 1:00 in the afternoon. He asked me to tell him what I thought he'd done wrong. I went over all the years of our marriage: owing people we couldn't pay and the I.R.S. and never being debt-free. I didn't mean having everything completely paid for - just able to make the payments. He agreed that was right. Then I poured out the ache of loneliness caused by his always putting me and the girls and our home in last place. He agreed he had done that too. We both wept until my whole body ached.

Then, assuming that he meant that God had taken the blinders off about everything, I told him that it was a false prophecy that brought this lady to "save the ministry". This prophecy convinced him that everyone else, including me, was of the devil and against him. I said, "You think everyone is trying to wreck your ministry so you don't have to listen to any of them. That prophecy has you convinced we don't have to repent of poor stewardship of God's money. The prophecy that told you to do that was TRUE! You've rejected the true for the false!"

I asked him to realize he had isolated himself from almost every friend he had who loved him. He was being controlled and manipulated. Ever since that prophecy, I had become the enemy, and my word didn't count for anything even though at that time I was still vice-president of the ministry. People were giving donations in the name of Born Again Marriages, which in people's eyes stood for me and him and a marriage ideal that we were no longer living. But when I would speak about this false prophecy, a wall would come up.

Finally I said, "God is a God of resurrection. If you leave the ministry to pay off the debts, God can resurrect it. God will respect our efforts to make restitution. If I could just hear you say, 'My God, I'm sorry that I can't pay these people back. God, please help me,' I would begin to respect you. You can't go on like nothing is wrong!"

Then he said that he had to go to the office at 1:00 and that he would be back after school to take Mandy to sell candy bars. He said he would make everything right and we two would go on together and make the ministry work. Part of me wanted to fling myself in his arms and believe him, but I had heard promises like this too many times. I said, "You do what God tells you, and I will watch. Maybe I'll begin to respect you and love you. I feel nothing except pain right now."

When he came back to the house three hours later he announced that he was going to his parents' home for the night. I asked, "Are you leaving after all that we talked about?"

My emotions were going up and down like a yo-yo. One minute he told me very unemotionally to go get a divorce. Then we went through a five-hour, gut-wrenching, crying-our-eyes-out session where I thought he'd decided to change.

I was trying to gear myself up to support him even though I felt dead on the inside. Now there was coldness and he replied, "I'm fasting, and I have to finish my fast and pray. I'm sorting things out." With that, he left.

I stood there in shock. I waited long enough for him to arrive at his parents' house. Then I called him. Crying, I said, "My emotions are shot, and I am a wreck. I thought that after our talk, you would spend a night at home. I thought we were going to try to see what it would be like without anger and tension in the house."

But all he would say was, "I'm praying and fasting. I'm not coming home."

I didn't hear from him again for about a week at which time he knocked on our door and said, "Here. I've been to a lawyer, and these are my terms. Now you go to your lawyer and draw up what you want."

"Kent," I said. "I have already been to see a lawyer, and I am not going to file for divorce. I have decided that it is absolutely against everything that I believe in. I am filing for separate maintenance, and I have legally resigned from the ministry. Maybe if you move out of the house, it will hit us both how serious this is. I will never file for a divorce. If you want it, you will have to do it all."

Kent said, "Fine. It is over, you know."

Then he left. I sat there and thought a while. I got up to call him but decided I wanted to look him in the eye. I got in my car, went down to his office, walked right in, and said, "Look me in the eye and give me a straight answer to one question. The God that woke you up and took the blinders off the other day and told you all the things that you were doing wrong and what you were supposed to do... what god was that? If it was God Almighty, you should be doing what He told you to do regardless of what I do. If I move to Tibet, you should be doing what God told you to do - if it was really God."

"Dru, **it is over!**" he said.

I said, "That is not what I asked you. Now answer my question. What god was it that woke you up?"

He finally said, "Okay. It wasn't God. It was emotion."

I didn't believe that because everything he said that day was Godly. The things that he had said that day could be backed up by the Scriptures. The prophecy that this woman got couldn't be backed up by the Scriptures. Neither could another prophecy concerning future ministry that he believed he had personally received after that one. He believed in it strongly enough to distribute typed copies to all the employees at the time. I was not given a copy. Much later an ex-employee played the tape for me and that was the first I'd heard about it. I said, "Okay. Was that the same "god" that manipulated my life with messages all of these years?"

He said, "Probably."

I left. What I'd been trying to do was make him see it wasn't right to say "God told me" one minute and brush it off the next minute, saying "It wasn't God." I was also trying to make him see that most of the "messages" he got were not from God.

There ensued a period when I felt like the last fourteen years of my life had been nothing but a failure. I had devoted my life to a marriage-healing ministry. Now my own was ending in divorce. I asked God to give me a burning bush under a fountain or a brick on the head. I asked Him to speak to me through His people or give me a "Rhema" from the Word or energize me with His faith like He did when I prayed Kent home the first time. "God," I cried. "If YOU want me to stand, I will stand! Just tell me that I am supposed to because I can't do it myself. I am so sorry."

Kristin and Peter.

13

GOD, NOW WHAT?

I threw myself totally on God's mercy. I prayed in the Spirit and asked, "God, what is Your will for my marriage? Am I supposed to stand **again**? Dear Lord, I need to hear from You."

I knew the first time Kent left that it was God who was giving me the faith to stand. That faith was not there this time. I felt like a fish out of water. I had thought that my whole calling in life was to stand and teach others to stand. I kept begging God to show me if that was what He wanted me to do once again. "Lord, You know I feel dead on the inside. I need You to give me some little flame of hope if I am to stand. So far, be it my fault or whatever, I can't get it. It is not here."

For months I went around feeling like a failure communicating only with close friends and my counselors. I was sure I'd lose all my friends, but instead, they held me up in prayer and with phone calls and invitations to eat out. I apologized to ministry workers, and when I opened up to them, we became closer than ever. Kent's relatives told me that I will always be a part of the family and that they love me. I will always love them, too. Kristin, Mandy, and I are closer than ever because no walls are between us. We aren't hiding a thing from each other. I am not trying to shelter them and thereby risk hurting them. We cry together about it.

Yet, there was such an overwhelming feeling of failure. For a long while, I thought that I had probably given up my only call from God just to be able to be my own person. The guilt almost dragged me down. I never wanted to fail God. I'd go through periodic depressions and wake up in the middle of the night shuddering in fear. I was afraid that if it came to my having to support Mandy, we'd end up out on the street without a penny. We had no savings or insurance, nothing but debts. I forced myself to pray in the Spirit instead of cry... when I could remember to.

Gradually, I noticed the depression periods DID always end and were coming less frequently.

One day I was talking with my friend, Jim Rumpf, who pointed out that Edison had proved ten thousand ways that a light bulb would not work. Then he said that some people might say that Edison had failed ten thousand times or they could say he had only proved ten thousand ways that it wouldn't work before he succeeded. Suddenly, a light bulb went on for me! Maybe my life wasn't a total failure. I had learned some things. I knew in a lot of ways ministry and marriage won't work. I was no longer in bondage to false doctrines and false prophecies. I was learning God loved me in the middle of my failures when I wasn't DOING anything for Him. The crippling inertia of failure began to lift, and a tiny flame of hope sprang up inside me. I didn't feel totally dead on the inside anymore.

Throughout these months, friends like Gavin and Patti MacLeod and several pastors I kept in touch with over the phone kept telling me, "You're going to write a book." A pastor I hadn't talked to in two years called out of the blue to say the same thing. I would always answer, "Who would want to read a failure story? People only want to read a success story. I don't have anything to write. My life is up for grabs."

All of a sudden, two days before Christmas, God spoke to me in the middle of a Bible study at my church: "Will you give Me a month to determine the rest of your life?"

I said, "Yes, Lord, I will do that," knowing that He meant I should fast and pray extra that month.

A few days later, to my amazement, I began waking up with the compelling urge that I **had** to write a book right in the midst of the crisis! I had to communicate to the people who followed our ministry and watched our show who don't know what has happened to me or the ministry. Just as I had longed to do when I learned of my errors, I was to help set free those who were in bondage to a doctrine I had perpetuated. Morning after morning I awakened with the urge to write NOW.

Finally I said, "God, if this is You, You will have to find me a publisher because You know I don't have a dime."

I made a phone call to an editor I had worked with on a book previously and told him my story. He said, "Dru, I'm out of the business, but I'm going to call a publisher who was my mentor and tell him your story."

Very shortly he called back with this publisher's unlisted phone number and said he wanted to talk with me. That is how I met Cliff Dudley.

After talking a while, he felt God urging him to publish my story. "But, Cliff," I said, "You need to know something. I don't have a dime to pay for it."

I think I "heard" Cliff smile on the telephone as he replied, "Dru, I always tithe every tenth book, and yours happens to be the tenth!"

In relating this almost bewildering chain of events to my friend, Lynn, she exclaimed, "Dru, how many more burning bushes do you need?"

I saw her point, but it seems God had one more "burning bush" in store for me. After Cliff and I talked to make sure that he knew my heart motives for writing and that we were in total agreement, I received my contract in the mail. I decided I would check with my friend, Pastor Blix, here in Council Bluffs for a final opinion as to whether this was indeed God urging me to write.

With my contract in my hand, I walked into his office. But before I could speak, he said, "Dru, I'm glad you called. I've had a message for you from the Lord for weeks now. Do you want to hear it?" Of course I did.

He said, "You are supposed to WRITE A BOOK RIGHT NOW!"

I think I managed to choke back the tears as I wordlessly handed him my contract.

During this period of re-evaluating my beliefs, I became like a baby Christian again. I felt so many of the things I had learned and had taught were out of balance. I really wasn't totally sure about anything anymore but my salvation. I started praying simple childlike prayers. In one instance, while Kent and I were separated, the ministry donations had fallen off so badly, that Kent could not give me any money for a few weeks. Kristin and Peter were coming home for a visit, and I didn't know how I was going to feed them. My sink faucet leaked so I had to keep it wrapped in a towel, and my toilet wouldn't quit flushing. My lawn mower was broken and my lawn was so high it was going to seed. Frustration and worry began to wear on my nerves. After fretting a while, I realized I couldn't do a thing about any of it. My only hope was God. I remember bowing my head on my kitchen counter, praying simply, "Lord, You know all these needs. Please take care of them. Thank You."

The answer came in dazzling swiftness. The next night my pastor, Jim McGaffin, knocked on my door. He said, "Hi, can't stay," and he handed me a check for $50.00!

I began jumping up and down screaming, "Groceries for Kristin and Peter!"

Jim looked at Mandy and said, "Does your mother always act this way?" and walked out.

The next day, Carol Sorenson came over. She used to see that all the letters written to the ministry got answered. She asked me why my faucet was wearing a diaper. Later she noticed the toilet wouldn't stop flushing. The following afternoon she appeared at my door with Rich Wilson, who programmed all the ministry computers. I found out he is equally handy at fixing sinks and toilets! And if this wasn't enough, two men from my church appeared at my door and announced they came to mow my lawn! Seems Pastor Jim had noticed it going to seed. My mind is always a little boggled when God takes such special care of me even when I'm not doing anything for Him... even when I've gone the other way and loused things up. I've learned He is my Father, and my Father loves me even when I make mistakes.

Since I trusted none of my old familiar doctrines, I did things I'd been taught mature Christians do not do - such as ask God for signs and tell Him I wouldn't move left or right if He didn't show me because I just didn't know anything anymore. And God met me right where I was with impressions from Him that I could check out with my counselors and the Scriptures. I was given supernatural gifts of money to help me give my daughters a beautiful Christmas, and with a car when it became obvious my old one needed replacing.

I would pray, "God, I'm walking on such new territory. I feel like such a failure, such a sinner because I have no faith to stand for the healing of my marriage. If I'm not so far outside Your will You can't even see me, please give me a sign so I'll know You're not displeased with me." (Before this, I was such a "faith" person. I'd have died rather than pray a prayer like that.)

Then I asked for $200 to go see Kristin and Peter. Three days later, within a two-hour time span on a Monday morning, my pastor and a friend, neither of whom knew my prayer, each put one hundred dollars into my hand! I cried and praised Jesus because I realized getting the exact sum, not a penny less or more, in such a supernatural time was not only the answer to my financial prayer but I knew without a shadow of a doubt, God was comforting me that I was not "so far out of His will that He couldn't see me." Time and time again when I was at such a low ebb, God would do things like this for me.

I learned to stop faking happiness. When someone asked me how I was, if I was scared and depressed, I said so without fear of displeasing God for not speaking in faith. HE knew I still had faith that He would snap me out of it, but I would express how I felt at the moment.

I've learned to relax and watch a favorite TV show with Mandy. When she says, "Mom, come cuddle me," now there is nothing more important to do than that.

When failure seemed all I'd achieved after fourteen years as a Christian, I realized I had my two wonderful daughters who loved me dearly and a new son (who was almost no trouble) who, when fear of poverty attacked me, said, "Mom, never worry about the future. I'll always take care of you."

When beautiful friends call me from all over the country to see how I am and tell me that they love me even though I haven't lived up to the image they had of me before I opened up... then I can thank God for these treasures that I'd not have without the past years' efforts. I have finally come to believe that because at present I have failed in my marriage and ministry, it does not make me a total failure now and forever. I have too many other blessings and my future is not over yet. God can bring victories out of calamities in each of our lives. It is a strong possibility He has one in store for me.

I know many ministers whose ministries look great but whose kids are a mess. Mine are beautiful and walking with the Lord. I don't regret the time I took away from the ministry to invest in my daughters. The joy of knowing that they love me unconditionally is greater than any public acclaim I may get from a ministry. I have the joy of knowing God has said to me regarding my mothering, "Well done."

I am now living through the reality of trusting God to supply all my needs, which I have told the Standers to do all these years. That was good teaching. I have opened myself to human criticism and made myself vulnerable to God. I am willing to wait for Him to reveal what His will for my future life is rather than rush into some man's idea - or what I might religiously think God's will is for me. I am sitting back, not moving, until I know it is God.

At this writing I feel that God still has things for me to do in His Kingdom. And once again He has stepped in to help me through a crisis that breaks my heart and makes me shudder in fear of the unknown just as He did for me fourteen years ago. I do feel an added happiness because I am becoming my own person, not compromising my own standards for anyone else. I am wondrously anticipating what God is going to do in my life. I've said I couldn't preach what I wasn't living. Now I can declare honestly from experience that when our whole life breaks asunder, a life we thought was tied up in a neat little package; when our every hope and dream crashes; when our reputation is ruined, and when everything we have trusted in goes awry, God is still God, and He will keep us when all else fails.

Once I cried out to God that it seemed unfair, almost cruel, to set us up as marriage ministers or even bring us back together at all if He knew it was going to crumble fourteen years down the line and break not only my heart but perhaps thousands who loved and believed in us. I don't have the answer to that, but I've learned that I must allow God to be right all the time. I must believe Ecclesiastes 3:1-3, "To everything there is a season... a time to heal, a time to break down and a time to build up." (Amplified)

Before you think I am using God for a cop-out for my failures, let me say I am not. I only know God is not my heavenly genie. I cannot dictate to Him by a "faith formula" how I'd prefer He handle my life - whether I understand why things went the way they did or not. I still believe God has a better plan for my life than I do, and I am going to trust Him to unfold it in His time.

14

BANKRUPTCY, DIVORCE, AND BURGER KING

As I end this writing, I have gone through bankruptcy and divorced - as of three months ago. Now I am working at Burger King.

During the beginning of this book, I would be too depressed to go home alone after I took Mandy to school in the morning, so I would go to my friendly, neighborhood Burger King. I would have breakfast, then because they had free refills on glasses of tea, I would spend hours researching and writing in my favorite corner of the atrium. One of the managers, Gwynn, would actually test new brands of tea on me, I drank so much!

One day, another of the managers, Tricia, said, "Dru, you're here so much. Why don't you come to work for us?"

I think she was half joking but when I found out I could get off at 3:00 and pick Mandy up at school at 3:30, I decided to give it a try. A real lesson in humility, maybe? It was quite a change from silk dresses on stage in Beverly Hills to bending over a hot broiler and steamer. I discovered I could work harder than I thought, and the job puts groceries on the table.

I work with some very nice friendly people who are very excited about this book.

Once I was in the dining room when a lady came up to me and said, "Dru Axtell! It is you, isn't it? I am from California and have followed your ministry. I am traveling through and wondered if there was any way I'd see you when I came to Council Bluffs. And here I find you at Burger King! God has blessings stored up for us in even the most unexpected places."

I really do not have a great-sounding end to this book. My future is still hanging in the balance. I do not have the vaguest idea what is going to happen to me. The depression and fear have almost vanished, which is a great triumph for me, and best of all I feel certain God is not through with me yet. I have gone from an attitude of despair and guilt to one of hope. I do know one thing for sure: I love Jesus MORE after all of this, not less. He has made Himself more real to me than ever.

I still go through agony when Mandy goes out the door to spend a weekend with Kent. The first time I almost went to pieces. Thank God for Christian friends. I can be working in the yard or doing almost anything and get a flash of, "Oh Lord, what have I done? No more family Christmases for Mandy and she's only ten." Remorse comes over me and I start the old "what-could-I-have-done-better" game.

It's mind blowing to find myself going through everything I fought so hard against in my ministry. I still care very much about Kent and all that has happened cannot erase the good times we shared and there were many.

I cried with my dear friend, Eva, who was our ministry pilot when she had to sell her airplane for peanuts because the engine was worn out. The ministry had promised to replace it but now, of course, there is no ministry and no money. She has turned it all over to God but I still feel so badly.

I don't know how God views all of this. I'm sure He was behind the miracles our ministry experienced. He provided us access to bring the good news to millions at a time via television - something Paul would have given his right arm to be able to do - and we blew it.

I guess I can't fully comprehend how much God loves me in spite of all my failures. One day as I was crying, asking God how He could forgive me again, my Bible fell open to Matthew 18:21, 22 where Jesus told His disciples they had to forgive seventy times seven. Then God said to me, "You don't suppose I'd ask anything of you I don't do Myself?" I wept in relief.

If discussing the mistakes that Kent and I made - the deception that we fell under, the false messages, the false submission, and putting the ministry ahead of everything else - can set other people free who are living the same way, then I say, "Thanks be to God."

If perhaps this book will caution others to be wise enough never to fall into those traps, then my life has not been a waste. I feel that a lot of pastors are going to lose their wives and kids if they don't stop being married to the ministry and shoving their families in the background - just working them in whenever it is handy. The family is the most important unit that God ever created. He created the family **before** the ministry. How we live in our home, where only Jesus watches, is what is important. **Our public life should just be an outgrowth of our private life**.

If you find yourself being drawn into television ministry, have your guard up against the glory getting to you. Remember, pride comes before the fall. Also, do not fall victim to the "Messiah complex" - thinking you are so powerful and special the rules do not apply to you.

I certainly don't want to underplay the many, many miraculous healed marriages that I have seen. Some time back, I was actually going to write a book called *A Hundred Healed Marriages*. I am thrilled with the miraculous healings that I have seen in our ministry, but I don't think that we need to continue justifying wrong praying, false doctrines and living in a fantasy in order to keep people "standing" for their marriage to be healed. God's witness to each individual is enough. Many couples who became associated with our ministry got their marriage healed before they ever heard of the Standers groups.

I trust that the edifying things that our ministry taught

will survive, but I want the cultishness and deception to be exposed and rooted out. One very important thing I have learned is: **GOD'S WILL IS NOT USUALLY SPOKEN TO US IN BLANKET STATEMENTS!** It is unwise to believe that He wants ALL marriages healed or that all sickness will be miraculously healed or that He hates every single divorce in the entire world. He doesn't hate the abused wife who gets knocked down the stairs every day for getting out of that marriage. Choosing to survive and be healthy and live to raise her children is using the brain God gave her. God doesn't hate that. He hates that it had to happen, but He DOES NOT hate her for getting free of a harmful husband. In fact, God does not hate us for getting a divorce even if we have wrong motives and His forgiveness is available to us whenever we come to Him with a repentant and contrite heart.

One day God shocked me by telling me I had served the god of the **institution** of marriage (meaning it was an idol to me) and I had to learn to serve **Him,** not an institution He had created for man's good. When we in our humanity blow it, God still does not sacrifice the person's welfare to preserve the institution. I believe just as the sabbath was created for man and not man for the sabbath, marriage was created for man, not man for marriage.

A friend of mine, who became Mrs. Nebraska recently, was divorced and met a Christian man who was divorced. They felt that God wanted them to get married. He died two years later of cancer. People from my ministry actually told her that her husband's dying of cancer was God's will because they had been married before and they shouldn't have ever married again. His death was their punishment from God, they claimed. When she told me, I apologized to her profusely. I really could hardly believe the hardness of heart that would cause anyone to presume to make such a judgment. I never wanted hurtful things like that to come out of my ministry. I hope this book will help prevent anyone from being wounded this way in the future.

Christians, of all people, should not say such unkind things to someone going through trauma. What is wrong with us? The world shows more pity and sympathy when people are experiencing tragedy than some Christians do. Sometimes we need someone to hurt with us, not tersely tell us to confess scriptures or arrogantly tell us it's our fault if a loved one dies. Mrs. Nebraska's husband died in her arms, and still she spoke healing Scriptures over his dead body. Whatever happened she operated in as much faith as she had and it is no one's duty to find fault with her. She did not need someone to pile guilt on her. That is not the heart of God who COMFORTS. I believe God is pleased with each of our attempts to walk in faith. And God doesn't want us hurting our fellow man's feeling in order to stick up for Him and make sure He doesn't look like a bad guy. God can stick up for Himself. Besides having mountain moving faith I believe we must be as a Job who said, "Tho He slay me yet will I trust Him." (Job 13:15)

We MUST get out of the bondage of losing all common sense to preserve someone's idea of what faith is! Each one of us must get our instructions from God and not try to live off someone else's revelation. They are examples of what God can do if He chooses. We must find out if He wants to do it that way or another way for us. Not doing so results many times in misdirected faith, ruined faith, even death.

But... no one should take this book as a license to quit working on their marriage and run off and get a divorce. If that is what you are getting out of this book, then you just want to see it that way. That is not my motive.

You need to seek God for direction in your marriage. Only HIS instruction for you will give you peace.

God doesn't want us in bondage to someone else's pet doctrine. He wants us free to hear from Him. "Now the Lord is the Spirit, and where the Spirit of the Lord is, there is liberty (emancipation from bondage, freedom)." (II Cor. 3:17) (Amplified)

As I began writing the closing chapter, a tornado ripped its way through our city. I had come home from work, changed out of my uniform and set off to run some errands when I heard over the radio that eight tornadoes had been sighted and downtown Omaha was being hit. We are right across the Missouri River from Omaha so I headed for home fast.

A dear Christian family moved into our neighborhood recently. They have a daughter, Laura, who is Mandy's age, and they are best friends. Mandy spends most of the time I'm at work at their house because Laura's parents have taken her in as practically one of their family.

I called their house to warn them of the tornado and tell Mandy to come home quick and found Laura's mother, Mary, had taken them to the mall! To say I was frantic is putting it mildly. The radio said high winds and flying debris were in downtown Omaha and it was minutes from there to Council Bluffs. I put the car in the garage, closed the windows, carried plants in, and PRAYED. I called two more times and still - no Mandy. I felt so helpless.

Just as the sky turned black, all the electricity went off, sheets of rain slapped furiously against the house, and branches snapped off like twigs, Laura's brother called and said they were home and all going to the basement! Thank you, God! Then the phone went dead! I wasn't going to go to the basement, but just then huge limbs crashed against the front of my house, and I realized they could come in my picture window. I grabbed a candle and headed for the basement. It was a lonely, scary time, huddling there, but I thanked God that Mandy and the Sumpters were home safe and thanked Him for saving my home.

At last most of the wind quit, and only sheets of rain fell. I noticed trees down as I scrambled into a raincoat to run down to Mandy. I had to go out the back door as my front door was blocked by a pile of branches. It was okay, though; the backyard fence had blown down so I walked right through! I met two firemen who said we were isolated because a huge tree had fallen across the street at the bottom of our hill! Mandy and I were doubly isolated because another had fallen across my driveway!

I found Mary with six crying, hysterical children. I told all the kids to start praising Jesus because our houses were all standing and they made it home just before the tree blocked our street. They did, and soon Mary and I and a bunch of tear-streaked kids ventured out to survey the damage with the rest of the neighborhood.

That evening frustration and panic began to set in. Even though I was so thankful to have my roof still over my head because many in our town didn't, I was supposed to have thirty people at my home for a wedding shower in three days! We had no phone, no electricity. No one could get in my driveway or front door, and all the branches were too big for me to budge an inch. And I didn't have money to hire anyone to help.

Mandy and I joined hands in the hundred degree heat and prayed a simple prayer by candlelight: "Lord, please send someone to help us clear the branches. Thank you."

Two hours later, phones came on and off sporadically, and one of the men from my church, who had mowed my lawn when my mower was broken, phoned and asked if we were okay. I said yes but we had branches down. Rich said he'd be over the next day to clear them. I said, "Oh, Rich, this is no small job. My front yard is covered, and they're big. We can't just pick them up."

"Oh, chain saw stuff, huh? Don't worry. I'll be there."

Mandy and I rejoiced. What an answer to prayer! Not only did Rich come the next day, but his wife Terry and three children and we all worked for six hours sawing, clearing, raking, and carrying wood to my wood pile. This family is Christian love in action.

The moral to this is not just that God is helping me since I'm alone. He is helping me **through** my church! I don't know how I'd have made it in and out of the horrid depression that hit me all this winter without my pastor's counsel. He knew me and he knew Kent. He loved our ministry, and he could empathize with my almost inability to cope with being the head of a nationally-known marriage-healing ministry and having my own marriage fall apart. Even though he hurt with me, he could still help me sort through it with Godly logic that I didn't have then.

Yes, we need to hear God's direction for our life, but we also need a shepherd to test whether what we think we've heard from God is off the wall or not. Our pastors love and care for us but can judge impartially and wisely what is of God and what is not of God when we are too emotionally involved in our own situation to know for sure.

Shepherds were given to us by God to keep us on the straight path, not running off on wild goose chases.

No one taught Kent and me the function of pastors, and we never submitted to one while in the ministry. We went to church all right, but thought we didn't need any kind of counsel by the pastor.

I am discovering the joy and comfort of being pastored for the first time in my Christian walk.

The Standers' groups certainly had a function, but if I'd known what I know now, each one would have been under the protective arm of a local pastor and church body. Standers' groups should not have been separate but incorporated as a function of a local church. There is the safeguard which would keep a cultish doctrine from getting a foothold. A wise pastor would spot it a mile off. He can also help decide if God is saying "Keep standing" or "You've stood and prayed long enough; you've done your duty before God; now go on with your life."

Just as I thought I had no more to share about how the Lord is helping through this, He chose to give another dose of His immeasurable unconditional love.

The morning of my birthday, Pastor Jim called to say the church wanted to treat Mandy and me to a spaghetti dinner that evening. When we arrived, I was ushered to the head table. Everyone sang Happy Birthday to me and I was presented with a decorated... watermelon! This really blessed me since only my heavenly Father knew that, as a child, the only thing I ever asked for on my birthday was a watermelon. Dad thought they were a waste of money but on my birthday, my Dad always gave me a watermelon. I accepted the melon, said the face on it looked just like Jim, and started to sit down. My pastor then said everyone wanted me to know they appreciated all the years I had been on the road for the Lord. There were healed marriages there because of our ministry. They wanted me to know I wasn't a failure because I was not presently in a big ministry. Then Jim said they'd taken up an offering for me and handed me a big handful of money... five hundred dollars! I choked up. I cried. I don't know if I was able to thank everyone adequately. The rest of the evening was a blur.

I was able to purchase Kristin and Peter's wedding pictures so I could put my favorite in this book and give the rest of the pictures to Kristin and Peter who'd been waiting fourteen months. I opened a small savings account and made the first house payment I ever made in my life **on time** all because of their love gift.

The love of God...will we ever fully comprehend it? I love you Jesus!

"For I know the thoughts and plans that I have for you, says the Lord, thoughts and plans for welfare and peace, and not for evil, to give you hope in your final outcome." (Jer. 29:11) (Amplified)

My pastor, Jim McGaffin, and me on my
birthday, with money the church gave me.